最后

名师名校名校长

凝聚名师共识
回应名师关怀
打造名师品牌
培育名师群体

图书在版编目（CIP）数据

核心素养视域下的高中英语语法教学研究 / 张莉著
. — 长春：东北师范大学出版社，2022.8
ISBN 978-7-5681-9260-6

Ⅰ. ①核… Ⅱ. ①张… Ⅲ. ①英语—语法—教学研究
—高中 Ⅳ. ①G633.412

中国版本图书馆CIP数据核字（2022）第141389号

□责任编辑：石　斌　　　　　　□封面设计：言之凿
□责任校对：刘彦妮　张小娅　　□责任印制：许　冰

东北师范大学出版社出版发行
长春净月经济开发区金宝街 118 号（邮政编码：130117）
电话：0431-84568023
网址：http：// www.nenup.com
北京言之凿文化发展有限公司设计部制版
北京政采印刷服务有限公司印装
北京市中关村科技园区通州园金桥科技产业基地环科中路 17 号（邮编：101102）
2022年8月第1版　　2023年1月第1次印刷
幅面尺寸：170mm×240mm　　印张：14.75　字数：248千

定价：58.00元

HEXIN SUYANG SHIYU XIA DE
GAOZHONG YINGYU YUFA JIAOXUE YANJIU

英语语法教学研究的

张 莉 ◎ 著

东北师范大学出版社

长春

我与"英语学习活动观"

——山重水复疑无路，柳暗花明又一村

《普通高中英语课程标准（2017年版 2020年修订）》提出了指向学科核心素养发展的英语学习活动观，明确活动是英语学习的基本形式，是学习者学习和尝试运用语言理解与表达意义、培养文化意识、发展多元思维、形成学习能力的主要途径。活动观的提出为整合课程内容、实施深度教学、落实课程总目标提供了有力保障，也为变革学生的学习方式、提升英语教与学的效果提供了可操作的途径。但是，我对学习活动观的认识经历了三个阶段。

一、初见——晦涩难懂

初知学习活动观是在2018年，当时学校聘请杨筱冰（正高级教师，陕西省特级教师，享受国务院特殊津贴专家，全国巾帼立功标兵，西安市有突出贡献专家。西安市人大代表，西安市红烛大使和年度教育人物，陕西省、西安市、碑林区三级杨筱冰中学英语名师工作室主持人，国家级和陕西省两级骨干教师）老师给我们做"教师专业能力提升之路"的报告，她讲到年轻教师要加强学习，提到了《普通高中英语课程标准（2017年版 2020年修订）》中的"英语学习活动观"。令人尴尬的是，作为教研组长的我竟然对此闻所未闻！讲

1

座结束后，我立刻在网上购买了这本书。当我手捧《普通高中英语课程标准（2017年版2020年修订）》时，感觉很陌生，里边提到的很多概念好像离我这个普普通通的一线教师太遥远，我感觉连读完课标的勇气都没有。然而，我深知作为我校高中英语组教研组长，我若不先读透课标，便没有底气和实力去指导或培训青年教师。为此，我又在网上买了一本《普通高中英语课程标准解读》，对着这个解读耐着性子逐字逐句地啃读，好像从最初的晦涩变得有点朦胧了，我慢慢明白学习活动观就是要求教师从课堂活动的视角重新审视课堂教学设计的合理性和有效性，整合课程内容，优化教学方式，为学生设计有情境、有层次、有实效的英语学习活动，通过这些贴近学生生活和有层次、有关联性的学习活动来推动学生的学习在课堂中真实发生，从而提升学生的课堂学习质量，助力于学生思维能力的培养。

二、再见——喜出望外

再见学习活动观应该是2019年的12月——接到陕西省第六批学科带头人培养对象的培训通知时。通知中说，2020年1月4日至7日陕西省教育厅和陕西省教育科学研究院组织集中培训，并要求各位学员思考自己的课题选题。我当时有点不知所措，原因是我以前从未独立完成过省级课题，这突如其来的重担和挑战，真的让我心里很没底。但我也努力思考了有关词汇、语法和高三一轮复习的课题研究方向。在跟导师沟通后，他建议我选择语法方向。在查阅了关于高中英语语法教学的一些文献资料之后，我喜出望外！现行语法教学多数采用的是讲授法、任务型教学法和情境教学法，没有任何涉及学习活动观的语法教学设计，于是我决定带领我的团队致力于这一方面的探讨和研究。

三、复见——喜忧参半

为了做好课题研究的准备工作，我开始着手认知和理解学习活动观。为此，我在工作坊的每篇公众号上发布与学习活动观相关的读书笔记，和同伴们一起讨论交流。此外，我还进行了三次"基于学习活动观的语法教学设计"的微培训活动。话说这三次培训，真是有辛酸和眼泪，更有感动和自豪！

第一次培训主要是基于课标中的概念表述。我讲得激情澎湃，但培训后收效甚微，老师们依然觉得云山雾罩。于是，我想光有理论上的培训是不够的，我需要让老师们直观地看到学习活动观到底该如何在课堂教学实践中落地。

再一次仔细地研读课标之后，我意识到基于学习活动观的教学设计应以促进学生英语学科核心素养的发展为目标，围绕主题语境，基于口头和书面等多模态形式的语篇，通过学习理解、应用实践、迁移创新等层层递进的语言、思维、文化相融合的活动，引导学生加深对主题意义的理解；帮助学生在活动中习得语言知识，运用语言技能，形成正确的价值观念和积极的情感态度，进而尝试在新的语境中运用所学语言和文化知识，分析问题，解决问题，创造性地表达个人的观点、情感和态度。以Book 1 Unit 4 Grammar — The Attributive Clause（that，which，who，whose）为例，我以描述中国的著名城市为主题，以四个具有关联性、实践性和综合性的学习活动为依托，信心满满地开始了第二次培训。本以为这次培训之后老师们肯定能将学习活动观理念植入各自的课堂教学中，但在老师们后来上交的教学设计中，我发现他们只是"穿新鞋，走老路"，沿用的仍然是任务型教学法和情境教学法，活动与活动之间毫无关联，也无整合输出。

苦苦思索之后，我开始筹划第三次培训。在第三次培训会上，我将课标上的概念表述变为自己的理解，把任务型教学设计或基于情境的教学设计与基于学习活动观的教学设计进行比较，通过改进使原有的任务型教学设计或基于情境的教学设计转变为基于学习活动观的教学设计，并告诉老师们学习理解类活动主要包括感知与注意、获取与梳理、概括与整合等基于语篇的学习活动，应用实践类活动主要包括描述与阐释、分析与判断、内化与运用等深入语篇的学习活动，迁移创新类活动包括推理与论证、批判与评价、想象与创造等超越语篇的学习活动。换言之，在学习理解类活动的基础上，教师引导学生围绕主题和所形成的新的知识结构开展描述、阐释、分析、判断等交流活动，逐步实现对语言知识和文化知识的内化，巩固新的知识结构，促进语言运用的内化，助力学生将知识转化为能力。在培训的最后，我尝试着让老师们以备课组为单位，以同位语从句为例，现场讨论，并分享所设计的主题语境及活动逻辑。

让我欣喜的是，在这次培训之后，老师们的思路都开阔了很多，所做的教学设计也非常精彩。在"基于学习活动观的语法教学设计说课大赛"的颁奖礼上，看着在台上领奖的小伙伴们，我觉得这既是他们的高光时刻，也是我的幸福时刻。这次活动不仅是他们的风采展示，更是我校高中英语教研组向学校提交的青年教师培养的合格答卷。每每空闲，欣赏着这些精彩的教学设计，我心中都有说不出的喜悦和激动！

"独行快，众行远。"我和我的团队在未来的日子里一定会一如既往地勤于钻研、相互扶持，以"研"为体，以"聚"合力，以"勤"克难。正所谓"艰难困苦，玉汝于成"，我们一定会在磨炼中成长为更好的自己，不负时光。

与杨筱冰老师合影

我与"深度学习"

  2020年10月12日，在陕西省教育厅、陕西省教育科学研究院的精心组织下，我有幸与一群心中有梦想的、优秀的陕西省教育同行共同奔赴杭州参加为期一周的培训学习。经历了疫情期的煎熬与等待，大家深知这次研修来之不易，并期盼自己能在这次学习中有所收获，期待这次学习能给自己以及自己的团队注入一针鲜活剂！

  10月13日早上8：30，我非常期待的讲座如期开始。本次讲座由来自上海师范大学教育学院的副教授、学习共同体研究学院的院长陈静静博士主讲。她是目前国内"深度学习"研究方面的领军人物。她的学术经历与工作经历可谓色彩斑斓：在十年的行动研究中，她深入课堂，精心研究三千多个课例，跟踪观察五千多名学生，跟随世界前沿学者与专家研学交流，著书立说。

  据她讲述，她致力于"深度学习"研究的根本动因是她发现我国学生的学习力正在急剧退化。更令人咋舌的是，学生学习力最充足的竟是学龄前与学龄期儿童！她非常渴望帮助广大一线教师理解学生真实的学习困境与需求，主张将传统的仅专注于教师教学的观察与评价的教研模式，逐步转向基于学生的课堂学习历程的课堂教研模式。

  为了更好地了解与洞悉学生的课堂困境，帮助学生实现从浅表学习到深度学习，教师要努力做到与学生合一，拆解学生学习的表面世界，从而进入学生学习的真实世界。课堂教研应从观察教师的"教"转向观察学生的"学"，从评价教师的教学能力转向对学生学习能力的观察与分享，从而真正了解学生的迷思概念与认知困境。

  解决学生虚假学习与浅表学习的关键是促进学生学习方式的变革。学生只有在自主、协同的氛围下进行深度学习，才能实现学习素养的养成与发展。在引导学生深度学习的过程中，教师的工作核心是学会倾听学生与自我反思，因为教师的倾听有重要作用：通过课堂内外对学生的观察，让学生把已知表达（书面或口头）出来；通过让学生提问等，了解个体学生的现有发展水平，分析预测出学生可能存在的学习困境与需求，从而为学生提供精准的专业支持与帮助。同时，学生之间也需要倾听，通过相互间的沟通、融合与分享，深化学习效果。

听完陈博士的讲座，我的内心久久不能平静。她直击课堂教学现状的痛点，尤其是高中阶段，越来越多的学生不愿参与课堂，学习力每况愈下，学习效率堪忧。思索再三，我想以目前高中英语教学中最耗时、低效的语法课堂为突破口，以高中英语必修课本中的23个语法项目为研究对象，设计一些优质的教学课例，旨在引导广大一线教师在日常教学中更好地践行和落实英语学科核心素养，使学习活动观和深度学习理论在课堂教学中真正得以贯彻和实践，从而促使学生的学习在课堂教学中真实发生。

与陈静静博士合影

目录
CONTENTS

上 篇 英语语法教学的历史与发展

下 篇 教学实践

上 篇

英语语法教学的历史与发展

　　英国语言学家威尔金斯说过："Without grammar very little can be convey ed, without vocabulary nothing can be conveyed."（没有语法，人们能表达的事物将寥寥无几；而没有词汇，人们无法表达任何事物。）这句话鲜明地指出了语言学习及语言学习中语法规则与词汇积累的重要性。英语语法包括英语词法和英语句法两个部分：英语词法主要是指英语单词的构成、变化和分类规律，英语句法主要是指英语短语和句子等语法单位的构成和变化规则。简单地说，英语语法知识就是用英语单词造句的规则系统，它是英语单词的构成规则、变化规则和组合规则的总和，是"形式—意义—使用"的统一体，与语音、词汇、语篇和语用知识紧密相连，是语篇意义建构的重要基础。语法知识运用的正确与否直接影响语言理解和表达的准确性和得体性。

第一章

英语语法教学的必要性和现状

作为学生的第二语言，英语这一独特而又庞杂的"符号系统"无疑容易给他们带来陌生感与疏离感。而在高中英语学习中，坚实的语法基础是英语水平进阶的充分和必要条件。语法作为英语学科知识的一部分，是学生语言运用能力的重要组成部分，是发展语言技能的重要基础，其重要性不言而喻。如果对于语法知识的掌握存在瓶颈，一旦突破，则会豁然开朗。

但是在目前的英语教学实践中，学生普遍感到英语语法难学、枯燥乏味，学习兴趣不高；教师深感语法难教，不仅耗时低效，而且大多数学生很难将所学到的语法知识运用到口语表达和写作实践中，从而导致语言输出质量不高。整体而言，英语语法学习难见成效，应该从教师和学生两个方面来归因。

一、教师的"满堂讲"

以教师为主体的语法教学方式使学生在课堂上被动接受信息，几乎不能真正参与课堂活动，结果导致很多学生死记硬背语法知识，综合运用语言的能力却极度低下。梳理语法教学历程，一线教师一直在竭尽全力改变语法教学收效甚微的现状，也努力尝试在语法课堂中运用任务型教学法、情境教学法等，这两种语法教学方式虽然有效提升了学生的课堂主体地位，学生的课堂参与度也明显增强，但也存在一定的弊端。例如，任务型教学中的"任务"和情境教学中的"情境"距离学生的生活实际比较遥远，由于活动的实践性不强，难以培养学生真实的语言运用能力，所谓目标语法项目的训练也只是被"嫁接"在虚拟的场景之中。同时，在任务型教学和情境教学中，课堂活动多是单线的、独立的。因此，活动之间的关联性较差，真正体现语言综合能力的课堂活动不足。

二、学生的"低参与"

学生"低参与"的根本原因在于以下三个方面：

1. 体系繁杂，易乱视听

就英语学科本身而言，语法知识体系繁杂，初入门径或者未得门径者难免思路混乱、不知所措。与汉语相比，英语中的词汇复杂得多。英语中的动词在时态方面就有一般过去时、一般现在时、一般将来时、现在完成时等多种时态的变形，而一个词加上前缀、后缀又可以派生出意义相关的新词。以句为单位来看，汉语中一般为主谓句或主谓宾结构，而在英语中则引入主系表的概念，并有主谓双宾、主谓宾宾补等；主从复合句涉及名词性从句、状语从句、定语从句等。学生在学习过程中很容易将这些概念混淆。笔者在执教时与学生沟通，有学生就坦言，一提到语法就"云山雾罩"，到处都是绊脚石。

2. 兴趣低迷，难下苦功

英语是学生的第二语言，因为远离生活情境，学生对其兴趣不高。在整个英语学习过程中，学生遇到了很多困难，如词汇的记忆、语篇的写作、听力的理解等，但最大的挑战还是语法的学习。对于很多学生而言，语法学习是枯燥乏味的，是难以理解的，这种挫败感进一步浇灭了其学习热情，并使其逐渐产生畏难心理。部分学生在英语学习中甚至直接放弃语法板块，并声称要从听力阅读中补回来。实际上，这种因畏难而生的逃避心理危害极大。在英语学习中，语法是绕不过去的，丢弃了入门的"钥匙"，又何谈"登堂入室"呢？

3. 学法不善，常入歧途

实际上，不少学生是有学习英语的动力的，他们也能在一定程度上坚持学习。不过，他们的理解可能还停留在浅表层次，认为英语语法的学习就是记住每个语法项目的结构就可以了，于是我们会经常看见学生手上拿着一本厚厚的语法书反复记忆，背诵语法书上所罗列的语法结构。但是我们也不难发现，这样学习语法的学生往往对语法系统一知半解，或者死咬概念，不知变通，导致在具体语境中对语法的实际运用能力存在很大的欠缺。这是因为学习方法出现了一定的问题，就如登高行远，知道去哪里很重要，而采取什么手段、借助什么工具也很关键。

第二章

英语语法教学研究的文献综述

一、引言

英语语法是英语语言的表达规则，而英语语法教学则是通过传递正确的英语语言知识，帮助学生明白和理解其形式及意义，从而达到在口头和书面表达中正确使用的目的。可以说，英语语法课堂教学是助力学生建构英语学科核心素养的主阵地。可喜的是，如今的语法教学已经不再采用"满堂讲"的传统语法教学模式，转而探求更加贴合新课标精神的新型语法教学方法。在几种目前常见的有别于传统的语法教学方法中，我们不难窥见方法设计者立足新课标的不同视角，他们对其中某些核心论点进行了深刻解读，从而设计了特别的环节，化解了传统语法教学模式中的某些"痛点"与"难点"。英语语法教学方法的演化史，就是广大英语学科教育工作者不断探索真理，不断继承和发展，追求语言教育本质的成长史。那么，什么是最佳的语法教学方法呢？可能只有在我们大致了解了当前几种主要的英语语法教学方法之后，才能得到答案。

二、现存主要的英语语法教学方法

（一）语法引导发现法

"语法引导发现法"又称"发现法"或"引导发现法"，源于美国教育心理学家布鲁纳于1973年在其著作《教育过程》中提出的概念。为了彻底解决传统语法教学只重视教师机械讲授与训练，不重视学生参与的"教学相离"问题，布鲁纳指出，学习需要学生积极主动地获取知识，从而主动发现知识的内在联系。语法引导发现法的学习过程是：教师首先创设与所教知识相关的问题情境，在解决问题的目标引领下，激发学生提出所有可能的有助于问题解决的猜想和答案，进而在这些猜想和答案中有目标地发现、解释、补充、修改和总结。语法引导发现法鼓励教师在语法课堂中尽量避免谈论让学生费解的抽象的语法术语，转而通过有意识地创设某种情境，让学生走入情境，观察、发现、总结出真实的语法现象，并做出适时的讲解和解释，帮助学生从抽象过渡到具体；再配合具有针对性的实践操作，让抽象的语法规则真正内化为学生自身的语言技能和知识。简言之，语法引导发现法的语法教学模式是"呈现—发现—练习—运用"。它有利于促进学生发挥学习的主观能动性和自身的学习潜力，通过主动发现洞见语法规则与语言本质，帮助学生建立内在的学科机制；其中明显增加的促进学生发现语法规则的教学活动，可以最大限度地调动学生的学习积极性，有助于学生享受发现知识的乐趣，激发学生的学习兴趣。

（二）任务型教学法

根据第二语言的学习和习得理论，英语的学习一定要涉及两方面的内容：一是在教学过程中激励学生进行有意识的学习；二是通过相关的交际活动，实际操练，让学生真正掌握这门语言。而建构主义认为，外语学习不能只依靠教师单方面讲授知识，而应该以学生为中心，让学生根据自身语言实际，在教师提供充足的补充资料（创设语言学习情境）的情况下，通过交际活动主动建构知识体系。因此，任务型教学法在语法教学中要求教师首先将具体的教学任务合理地分配给学生，让学生首先建立起对即将学习的语法知识的整体认识；其次，按照任务特点，将学生分成对应的任务小组，让学生通过对各自任务的合作探究过程深入理解相关语法知识点，并形成一定的学习计划和总结，向全班汇报任务的完成情况；最后，设置足够的情境交际活动，帮助学生完成语法交际练习，将语法规则运用到实际操练中。任务型教学法强调学生的主体作用，能够最大限度地调动学生的学习积极性和参与性，有助于学生在习得英语语法知识的同时提高解决问题的能力。同时，一系列的任务设置能够将沉闷的语法规则学习转化成一个个生动的任务"闯关"活动，大大提高英语语法学习的趣味性，而这一点正是传统英语语法课堂最难企及的高度。

（三）情境教学法

情境教学法是新课程改革"在真实情境中学习英语语法"要求的产物。情境教学法指导下的英语语法教学，要求授课教师在教学之前对既定的语法教学内容进行分析和加工，像"导演"一样，把枯燥的语法知识编排进生动有趣的情境之中，在课堂上把学生引入其中，让他们在特定的情境中观察、感受、发现，并学会运用语法知识。运用情境教学法的语法教学课堂更像是一出被精心设计的戏剧，学生既是"演员"也是探索者，他们被置于充满知识性的舞台上，各自发挥主动性，在好奇心的驱使下与其他小伙伴通力合作，并进行独立思考，在发现问题和解决问题的过程中自然而然地习得原本抽象冗杂的语法规则。情境教学法将英语语法教学置于一个真实完整的英语情境之中，为语言赋予了生命力，给语法规则提供了肥沃的土壤，大大降低了学生的接受难度，满足了学生的心理需求，提高了英语语法教学的生动性，激发了学生的学习兴趣，提高了学生解决问题的能力，极大地促进了学生英语学科素养的全面发展。

（四）合作学习法

为了摆脱传统语法课堂教学中教师"一言堂"的困境，打破长久以来语法知识被固化为枯燥的条条框框的束缚，提高英语教学质量，更为了提高学生的语法学习兴趣和关注学生学习本身，合作学习法被引入到英语语法教学中。合作学习法的重点是将教学班级合理编组，以不同小组为单位进行教学。每个小组、小组内的每名组员均要分工明确，各司其职，在完成各自的学习任务的同时兼顾小组其他成员和整个小组，甚至其他小组的学习活动，通过交流与合作，共同探讨完成整个学习任务。在语法操练环节，教师根据实际情况开展以小组为单位的实践活动，如小组竞赛活动，鼓励小组成员群策群力，并按照整体成绩进行评价，体现团队优势。合作学习法鼓励学生"在做中学、在学中做"，真正让学生行动起来，做语法课堂的主人。合作学习法顺应当今时代"合作才能发展"的主流认知，允许学生在语法课堂上明确自身角色，积极主动地借助同伴帮助和小组合作，感受伙伴们对于同一语法知识不同认知的思想碰撞，从而相互学习。整个过程不断激励学生在团队中学习与探究、合作与成长，使其取长补短，形成团队内部的竞争与合作意识，让学生不仅习得了语言知识，更提升了学习与社会生存能力。

（五）基于语篇的教学法

《普通高中英语课程标准（2017年版）解读》中指出："语言运用视角使我们意识到，语言运用不仅仅需要传统意义上的语言本体知识作为其基础，还需要运用型知识，即需要语篇和语用知识，来盘活语音、词汇和语法知识。"语法教学有三方面的内容——语法的形式、意义和运用（form, meaning and use）。没有在有效语篇中探讨的语法规则缺乏存在的土壤。基于语篇的语法教学在内容和语境的结合下充分利用语篇中的语法形式、意义和语法运用的资源，集中时间，集中材料，探讨特定语篇中的有效语法规则，逐步深入，使学生有意识地学会某一种情境下的语法知识。基于语篇的语法教学在帮助学生习得语法知识的同时，还将语篇中的文化背景知识、跨学科知识、英语思维方式及语言运用方法教给学生，让他们犹如走进一个由英语语言搭建起来的奇幻世界。在这里，他们不仅可以感受英语语言的魅力，在真实场景中习得语法规则，更有机会领悟到跨学科知识，感受原汁原味的英语思维和外来文化，极大地促进他们文化意识、思维品质和学习能力的提升。

（六）"翻转课堂"教学法

为了适应日新月异的信息化时代，享受互联网红利为英语语法教学带来的便利，也为了克服传统语法教学"重传授，轻内化"的弊端，"翻转课堂"教学法应运而生。即在课前，由教师提供与课程相关的学习资源（例如微课等视频材料），学生自主观看视频学习课程内容，而在课堂上则由师生共同进行作业答疑、合作探究以及迁移运用，学生在教师的指导下完成知识的理解、内化与总结。简言之，"翻转课堂"教学法将传统的语法课堂上的习得和内化环节互换顺序，以培养学生的自主学习能力，强调语法知识的内化过程。这一方法将较易操作的语法识记环节放手交给学生，在课堂上集中力量处理语法运用问题，极好地落实了语法教学的课后理解与内化环节，通过教师参与学生的答疑、讨论、分辨、探究等活动，提高了学生英语学习的主人翁意识，锻炼了学生之间的合作交流能力，培养了他们的团队协作意识，真正践行了"以学生为中心"的教学理念，发展了他们独立思考的能力，为英语语法教学课堂注入了活力。"翻转课堂"教学法是英语教学在"互联网+"时代顺应潮流，不断发展的成果，将互联网资料融入日常的语法课堂，让学生在搜集资料、学习资料、深化知识的过程中掌握语法学习的主动权，并增强学习的使命感，在提高课堂学习效率的同时发展了学生的学习能力，从而将新课标提倡的发展核心素养的目标落到实处。

（七）"显隐性相结合"教学法

随着英语语法教学重要性的不断突出，围绕着如何讲授英语语法的问题，一线教师与学者之间长期存在着以"形式"与"意义"为焦点的争论。传统语法教学认为，语法教学应当以注重语法形式的"外显"方式为主，教师首先将语法规则通过演绎的方式直观地呈现在学生面前，然后就所讲述的内容让学生进行大量的相关练习，以印证、熟悉所学语法规则。外显法有助于基础较薄弱的学生快速掌握新授语法知识的基本内容，但是有着显而易见的缺陷，教师大量灌输的语法课堂经常让学生昏昏欲睡，甚至望而生畏；学生机械训练，甚至背诵毫无意义的规则性文字，缺乏必要的口语训练，导致学生在实际交际中不敢开口。鉴于此，20世纪80年代后期，以重视学生的主体地位、强调语法教学应注重语言的意义表达、培养学生交际能力为核心的交际教学法应运而生，但是它走向了外显性语法教学方式的另一个极端。交际教学法与外显教学法理论对立，在语法教学中采用归纳法，通过训练学生的语言交际能力，让学生自己去内化和体会对应的语法规则知识，语法教学的重点在于让学生通过内容去理解形式，将语法知识讲解从课堂上隐去，故而也被称为"内隐教学法"。内隐教学法确实提高了学生的表达能力，但是其对于语法规则"不求甚解"的处理方式，导致学生在语言表达的准确性，特别是书面表达能力方面存在很大问题。至此，两种截然对立的英语语法教学方法引起了外语教育界的广泛关注。通过对大量教学实例和对比实验结果的深入分析和研究，我们得出这样的结论：外显教学法和内隐教学法并非互相对立，二者可以相互补充，共同服务于英语语法教学，即"显隐性相结合"教学法。"显隐性相结合"教学法集显性和隐性教学法的优势于一身，并做出了适当调整，让二者的优势得到最大限度发挥的同时避免了各自的缺陷。教师首先设置包含目标语法知识的场景，让学生接触鲜活的语言材料，在真实场景中分组讨论并归纳该语法规则的一般知识；然后教师集中讲解，呈现该知识，通过对比让学生明确意识到自己在归纳学习中存在的问题，及时调整并认真巩固该语法知识；接着教师为学生准备足量的口头和笔头练习，让学生围绕目标语法知识进行不断的交际练习，并在这一过程中进一步内化和巩固语法知识。"显隐性相结合"教学法让课堂经历了"隐性教学—显性教学—隐性教学"的过程，使整个课堂动静结合、内外兼修，能较好地提升学生的英语语言能力。大量一线教师的教学实践证明，"显隐性相结合"教学法不仅可以帮助学生夯实基础的语法规则，而且可以明显提升学生的口语及书面表达能力。

（八）沉浸式教学法

英语课程的总目标是培养学生的综合语言运用能力，提升学生的核心素养。但是对于中国学生而言，在汉语思维已经根深蒂固的情况下，他们的英语思维能力培养难度可见一斑。如何在强大的母语环境下培养英语思维，发展外语的语用能力，是我国英语教育工作者长期思考的问题。正如语言学的观点："英语不是学出来的，是用出来的。"起源于加拿大魁北克省的沉浸式教学法开创了一种全新的外语教学模式，解决了克服母语干扰，自然习得外语的难题，并取得了丰硕的成果，值得我国英语教育工作者借鉴。沉浸式教学法，顾名思义，就是让学生"浸泡"在英语环境之中学习英语，暂时忘掉汉语，教师在课堂的各个环节充分创造机会，让学生持续接受英语语言的刺激，保持大量的英语语言输入，从而使学生在这个刻意营造的良好的英语语言环境中自然而然地习得英语语法知识，形成英语语言思维，达到灵活运用英语语言的目的。沉浸式语法教学建议教师全英文讲授语法课，为学生营造英语语言的"浸入"环境。课前，教师可以安排学生充分利用3～5分钟做一个简短的Duty Report，选取学生感兴趣的日常话题，让学生用英语进行讨论，激发学生学习英语的兴趣，丰富学生的英语文化知识，并对接下来的英语语法课起到较好的热身作用。课堂中，教师尽可能创设英语语言情境，让学生走进一个个英语小故事及有趣的英文情节之中，加强各个学习小组之间的口语交流，并让其反复操练。交流内容不限于特定的情节，也可以是相互问候或本节课的学习心得和学习感悟等。如果学生在口语交流中学生遇到问题，教师要鼓励学生不怕犯错，积极向优秀的同学和教师请教学习，让学生完全沉浸在英语的世界里，让英语语法学习自然而真实地发生。课后，教师可推荐学生尽可能多地接触英文原版电影、英文歌曲，鼓励学生多看英文报刊，多听英语电台广播，全方位、多角度、源源不断地接受英语语言刺激。这些语言刺激可以帮助学生从无意识的语言输入过渡到有意识的语言输入，从而自然而然地学会地道的英语表达和英语思维，形成英语"语感"，最终达到利用所学语法知识流利表达自己观点的目的。

（九）PPP教学法

根据二语习得经典理论，"Learning is focused on rules which are then automatized as a set of habits."，英语语言学习实际上是一个循序渐进的积累而后产出的过程。PPP教学法就是这样一种遵循从积累到产出的规律的语法教学方式。PPP教学法以语法学习的三个阶段命名，分别是Presentation（演示）、Practice（实践）、Production（成果）。在Presentation阶段，教师需要通过阅读、听音、讨论等形式对目标语法内容进行呈现、解释和演示，让学生对新授语法知识有充分的认识和了解。教师要尽可能地充分解释，让学生主动意识到语法知识与自身需求之间的关系，引起学生对新授语法知识的兴趣，激发学生的求知欲。在该阶段教师是课堂活动的主导者，主要承担讲解任务，学生的主要任务是关注教师讲解的内容，并主动建立起新旧语法知识之间的关联。在Practice阶段，学生在教师的指导下就第一阶段讲授的语法知识进行大量的针对性练习，包括用适当形式填空、句子转换、句子配对、翻译、口头对话、书面表达等形式。总之，在此阶段，教师要尽可能鼓励学生运用所学语法知识完成各类练习活动，巩固所学，夯实基础；注意发现重难点，并及时纠正错误和查漏补缺，力图将学生对目标语法知识的认识从感性阶段上升到理性阶段。在这一阶段，学生自主学习和合作学习是课堂的重点，教师是课堂活动的观察者，是学生学习的助手。在Production阶段〔又被称为自由学习阶段（free stage）〕，教师鼓励学生完全摆脱语法知识性内容的束缚，更加自由地借助语法规则用创造性的方式将新旧知识相融合，表达自己的观点，如情景会话、角色扮演、戏剧模仿等，完成高质量的语言输出，从而正确理解语法规则以及英语语言的特点。在这一阶段，学生已经成为课堂的主导者，在接受足够的语言输入和大量练习的前提下，他们可以灵活运用语言，完成知识的内化与运用。通过PPP教学法的三个阶段，我们可以看出教师和学生的地位在不断发生变化，教师的作用随着课程的深入在不断淡化，而学生则由被动的知识接受者转变为灵活使用语法知识的课堂主导者，符合学生"接受—理解—掌握"新知识的规律。在整个课堂中，学生不仅看到了自己语法知识的增长，更看到了自身英语语言运用能力的提升，有利于增强学生英语学习的自信心。同时，PPP教学法让教师对语法课堂充满掌控感，其框架式的教学模式和教学结果可评可测的优势可使经验欠缺的新任教师容易掌握，避免了教学经验不足导致语法课堂步骤错乱等问题，大大保证了他们的语法教学质量。

（十）思维导图教学法

新课标提倡英语教学注重培养学生以思维品质等为重点的英语学科核心素养。思维品质被界定为一个人的"思维个性特征，反映其在思维的逻辑性、批判性、创造性等方面所表现的能力和水平"。在英语学科中培养和发展学生的思维品质，就是通过教学引导学生关注语言与文化现象，归纳英语语言的特点，帮助学生学会运用观察、比较、分析、推断、归纳、评价、创新等思维方式，提高学生的学习效率和学习能力。然而，传统的线性语法讲解和笔记法，只会将学生的思维禁锢在枯燥、冗杂的描述性文字中，使学生的思维只能在一行一行的文字表述中缓慢前行，极大地限制了学生发散性思维能力的培养，遑论较高层次的逻辑思维、推理判断思维能力的成长。思维导图教学法的引进仿佛给中国半个世纪的传统语法教学打开了一扇窗，仿佛给课堂安上了X光机器，让原本深奥难懂的语法思维清晰明了地呈现在每个学生的眼前，即实现了语法思维可视化。这样，语法知识就像我们生物课上第一次通过显微镜观察植物叶片那样让人惊奇，每一条语法规则都像根根分明的叶脉那样被清晰地呈现在相应的脉络之中。

思维导图教学法运用图文并茂的方式，把目标语法知识用生动的线条、简洁的词语、丰富的色彩呈现在学生面前，能迅速吸引学生的眼球，并且清楚地呈现出语法教学的重点，让学生过目难忘。比起传统的线性讲述英语语法的课堂，思维导图教学法可以让学生有效地将思维过程与语法关键词相结合，轻而易举地抓住语法知识的重点，更易记住所学知识，提高学习效率。线性语法教学最难克服的困难就是随着学生学习的语法知识的增多，旧的语法知识就像其记忆仓库里的陈年旧物一样被搁置起来。久而久之，越来越多的语法知识停留在记忆中的某个角落，难以被提及，导致新旧知识断层，遗忘率高。而思维导图教学法强调建立起完整的语法知识体系，将相关语法概念的每一个细小分支都尽可能全面地纳入到一张完整的语法脉络图中。在一张以某个语法点为核心的思维导图中，学生不仅可以详尽、清晰地一眼识别相关知识细则，更能够通过线条关系，梳理、关联、对比新旧语法知识，有效地做到新旧知识内化，并提高思维能力。更难得的是，思维导图教学法倡导发散思维的尝试和运用，可以有效激发学生的想象力与创造力，从而有效地提升学生的创新性思维能力。

三、总结

以上十种常见的英语语法教学方法各有所长，都体现了广大一线教师在新课标、新理论的指引下不断思考、勇于探索、追求卓越的工匠精神。他们为追求更加完美的新型语法课堂，做出了一系列珍贵尝试。这些方法都立足于"以学生为中心"的科学教育理念，力图在提高学生学习兴趣，全面发展学生学习和思维能力的同时，克服传统英语语法课堂的种种缺陷，打造更加生动、有趣、高效的英语语法教学课堂。然而，若问哪种方法才是英语语法教学的"金科玉律"，笔者相信"学无止境，教无止境"。随着广大英语教学者对新课标研究的不断深入以及对英语语法教学课堂理解的不断深化，更完善的英语语法教学方法会不断涌现。它们必将集众家之长，立足新高度，解决新问题，成为更加精准地阐释新课标精神的新成果。

参考文献

[1]周遥.中学英语语法教学探索［D］.上海：华东师范大学，2007.

[2]胡月.情境教学法在高中英语语法教学中的应用探讨［J］.农家参谋，2020（3）：264.

[3]张维红.任务型教学法在高中英语语法教学中的应用［J］.文学教育（下），2016（2）：68.

[4]朱晓东，范雪梅.语法引导发现法下的高中英语语法教学实践［J］.山东师范大学外国语学院学报（基础英语教育），2015（5）：62-67.

[5]陈纪泽，夏俊梅.翻转课堂在高中英语语法教学中的应用——以强调句学习为例［J］.海外英语（上），2018（2）87，91

[6]唐汶.PPP教学法发展研究综述：优势与挑战［J］.陇东学院学报，2017（3）：114-117.

[7]季淑凤，葛文峰.显性与隐性结合下的英语专业学生语法学习动态平衡研究［J］.安康学院学报，2016（2）：120-123.

[8]傅向萍.沉浸式教学法在初中英语教学中的实践和研究［J］.校园英语，2019（12）74-75.

[9]董昕.沉浸式教学法在大学外语教学中的应用研究［J］.黑龙江畜牧兽

医，2017（5）：267-269.

［10］王丹.任务型教学法在小学英语语法教学中运用的行动研究——以延吉市某小学为例［D］.延吉：延边大学，2016.

［11］蔡文娟.英语语法能力培养的原则与方法［J］.文学教育，2013（1）：60-61.

［12］刘忠政，李西.近12年国内英语语法教学研究综述与前瞻［J］.（外国语文四川外国语学院学报），2010（3）：122-125.

［13］孙鹏.英语任务型教学与PPP教学模式结合运用的理论与实践［J］.现代教育管理，2009（4）：85-87.

［14］张芒.高中英语语法教学中思维导图应用研究［J］.中学生英语，2020（16）：112.

［15］唐文化.高中英语语法教学中抽象思维能力培养初探［J］.英语教师，2019（18）：138-139，153.

［16］郑就.巧用思维导图培养学生核心素养［J］.教师博览（科研版），2019（3）：59-60.

［17］Rod Ellis. Task-based Language Learning and Teaching［M］. Oxford：Oxford University Press，2003.

［18］Scott Thornbury. How to teach grammar［M］. Harlow：Longman，1999.

第三章

英语语法教学的理论依据

第一节　建构主义理论

　　建构主义是20世纪80年代起逐渐兴起的一种新的学习观。该学习观既是认知主义的延伸，又是一种最能与素质教育理念相吻合的教学理论，其代表人物主要有皮亚杰、科恩伯格、维果茨基、斯滕伯格以及卡茨。最初的建构主义主要以儿童为研究对象，指出儿童对外部世界的认知是在与周围环境的相互作用下慢慢建立起来的，并且在此相互作用的过程中，儿童自身的认知结构也会获得极大的发展。对此，在发展领域中最具影响力的皮亚杰在先期建构主义的基础上，将该观点衍生到了两个层面，即"同化"与"顺应"。其中，同化是指个体将外界刺激所提供的信息整合至自身认知结构的过程，而顺应则是指个体原本的认知结构受外部刺激影响而发生改变的过程。此外，皮亚杰还认为，人的认知结构是经历了大量的同化与顺应才逐渐构建起来的，认知结构的提升则经历了"平衡—不平衡—新的平衡"这样一个不断循环的过程。

　　基于皮亚杰的研究理论，科恩伯格又对认知结构的性质以及发展条件等进行了更为深入的研究，并提出个体的主动性才是其建构认知结构的关键。另一个构建主义的重要研究者维果斯基则认为学习者所处的社会文化历史背景将是影响其认知结构形成的关键。对此，维果斯基还明确提出了两种个体发展水平，即现实发展水平和潜在发展水平。其中，现实发展水平是指个体独立活动时所体现出的水平，潜在发展水平则是指个体受到成人或比他成熟的个体的帮助所能达到的水平，而位于现实发展水平与潜在发展水平之间的区域便是我们熟知的"最近发展区"。

斯滕伯格和卡茨等人强调在建构主义认知过程中个体的主动性起到关键性作用，并对认知过程中如何发挥个体的主动性做了认真的探索。

建构主义理论的内容极为丰富，但其核心内容可概括为：以学生为中心，强调学生对知识的主动探索以及主动构建、发现所学知识的意义。与此同时，建构主义还认为知识不应仅局限于教师的传授，学习者应当基于自身成长的不同社会及文化背景借助教师的帮助来构建。当然，在此过程中，由于学习必须基于一定的情境，"情境""协作""会话"和"意义建构"等均是学习环境的不同属性。对此，我国学者何克抗同样指出，建构主义所提倡的应是基于教师指导、以学生为中心的教育环境。在此过程中，教师并非知识的传授者，而是学生学习意义建构的帮助者；学生也并非知识的被动接受者，而应该成为信息加工的主体，承担起知识意义建构的责任。

在建构知识的过程中，教师应该是重要的引导者，要在英语语法课程的教学过程中充分发挥指导性作用：一是教师应该采用多元化的教学策略来激发学生的学习兴趣，让学生能够更加主动地投入到英语语法学习当中，促使学生在英语语法课程中形成良好的学习动机；二是教学活动的设置应该在学生已有知识的基础上结合新的教学内容进行综合，目的是帮助学生尽可能地将之前所学习的语言知识联系起来，从而使其逐步形成完善的知识体系；三是教师应该组织学生进行协作学习，并给予学生一定的指导和帮助。

建构主义理论明确强调了学习者先思考后融入学习情境的重要意义，这样才能够在日常学习过程中掌握丰富的学习经验，才能够在遇到尚未接触过的问题时凭借自身的经验进行解决；在遇到接触过的问题时根据自己之前总结的经验进行处理，从而提出解决问题的有效策略。因此，教师在教学过程中不能忽略学生已经掌握的知识经验，要强调对学生认知能力的提升，让学生能够凭借以往的知识经验掌握更多的英语知识，逐步生成新的知识。但是，教师不能片面地将教学过程看作知识传递的过程，而应该将这个过程视为处理知识的中转站。同时，教师在课程中的知识传授并不具备权威性，而应该重视学生在课程学习过程中对相关知识的理解。

学生在课堂教学过程中的角色是知识获得的重要参与者和建构者。在建构主义理论中，学生需要真正融入学习情境，在良好的教学情境中更好地完成学习任务，逐步将自己所学习的语言知识结合起来，从而形成系统完善的知识体系。

总之，要想促使学生在高中英语语法学习中成为知识的主动建构者，教师在其学习过程中应努力做到以下两点：一是通过设置与学生生活实际相关联且包含目标语法知识的课堂活动，为学生使用发现法和探索法进行语法知识建构创造条件，以帮助学生感知和体验语法的形式和意义；二是通过设置由浅入深、层层递进的具有关联性和综合性的课堂思维活动，帮助学生营造语法知识的使用环境，使学生在语言的使用中学习、成长，从而达到真正掌握语法知识的目的。

第二节　合作学习理论

有关合作学习，我国古代的典章制度专著中便曾提出过"相观而善之谓摩"的观点，该观点的大意是学习应经过必要的切磋与交流，如此方能达到共同发展的目标。如今，在我国教育界广为熟知的合作学习理论则是在20世纪70年代由美国著名教育学家David Koonts提出的。其常见的运用策略是将2～6名具有不同学习能力的学生组成一个学习小组，小组成员通过相互督促与合作共同完成小组学习目标，进而达到共同进步的目的。合作学习模式在教育领域中的运用与个体学习之间最大的区别在于，合作学习不仅有助于学生内在竞争意识的激发，而且能够使资源的利用更加充分。此外，教师的传统角色定位也将得到相应的改变，如在基于合作模式的高中英语语法课堂中，教师便由传统的知识传授者变成了学生学习的促进者。当然，针对合作学习，国内外学者也进行了大量的研究工作，指出成功的课堂合作学习应当包含五大要素，即小组成员之间积极的相互依赖关系、个体及小组责任、师生之间的人际交流与小组合作技能、面对面的促进和影响以及小组自评。而D.W. Johnson，R.T. Johnson，等学者基于合作学习的内涵提出了最有利于学生竞争、平等意识激发的合作学习模式，包括问题式合作、表演式合作以及讨论式合作。此外，罗莎在其所发表的研究报告中指出，合作学习策略不仅有助于学生学习兴趣的激发，而且能突显学生在学习中的主体地位，进而有助于提升学生的主体意识，发展学生的英语思维能力。

合作学习是一种富有创意和实效的教学策略。由于文化背景、教育教学条件、具体实施方案等方面存在差异，各学者对合作学习基本含义的看法各不相同。

美国专家认为，合作学习是在小组中进行学习活动，根据小组成绩给予奖励的一种教学模式。我国研究学者则认为，合作学习是以学习小组为基本形式，以团体评价为标准，共同完成教学目标的一种教学活动。尽管各学者对合作学习的描述各不相同，但笔者认为，合作学习是学生以小组的形式进行学习活动，以小组整体表现和团体成绩作为评价标准，以塑造学生的心理品质、培养学生的合作意识、提高学生的学习成绩为目标的一种教学策略。它主要包括拟定学习目标、组建学习小组、组织分工合作、制定评价机制四个环节。

小组合作学习模式是一种将创意与实践相结合的教学策略，充分体现"以教师为主导，以学生为主体"的理念，为学生提供自主学习的空间、创造合作学习的平台；通过在课堂上注入新元素（小组合作教学模式），丰富课堂形式，充分调动学生的学习兴趣。在传统的教学模式中，学生参与度不高，只有少数学生发表自己的意见，大多数学生成为旁观者。小组合作学习模式能让课堂由一个活动点变成若干个活动点（不同的小组），便于学生交流，为学生营造轻松的学习氛围，提高学生的参与度拓展学生展现自我的空间，让学生在学习过程中收获快乐与成效。

简而言之，小组合作学习模式是一种有效的学习策略，它能为学生提供交流机会、创造学习氛围、搭建展示平台，对于培养学生良好的人际关系和团队合作意识具有重要意义。

我国对于合作学习的研究始于20世纪80年代末。进入20世纪90年代以后，关于小组合作学习的研究和试验便逐步推进。随着新一轮基础教育课程改革的实施，各中小学纷纷采用小组合作学习模式进行教学实验，在全国掀起了小组合作学习模式的实验热潮，如杭州大学教育系的"个性优化教育的探索"、山东省教育科学研究所的"合作教学研究与实验"、湖南师范大学教育系的"协同教学实验"以及北京师范大学教育系的"少年儿童主体性发展实验"等。

山东省教育专家王坦在其论作《合作学习的基本理论与实践研究》中阐述了合作学习的一些基本概念，并对小组合作学习的课堂实践给出了理论指导和实践建议。他指出，合作学习是以小组活动为基本教学形式，以团体成绩为评价标准，以提高学生学习成绩、改善班级学习气氛，促使学生形成良好的心理品质和实践能力的一种富有创意的教学策略。

通过文献研究发现，我国较早的实验小组合作学习模式出现在浙江省杭州市。采用小组合作学习模式授课的教师认为，传统的教学模式太单一，导致大多数学生对学习失去兴趣，成为课堂的旁观者；小组合作学习模式将课堂教学由一个活动点变成若干个活动点，可以提高学生的参与度，给课堂带来新的生机与活力。近几年，国内小组合作学习的理论逐渐趋于成熟，部分学校开始试行小组合作学习，并相互交流实践经验，不断挖掘小组合作学习的实用价值，逐渐带动各中小学在教学中采用小组合作学习模式。

国内关于小组合作学习的研究范围涵盖了合作学习理论基础、合作学习的理论指导与实践建议、合作学习的操作与反思、合作学习中的人际关系和交往等内容。相关实验和研究对小组合作学习的理论基础、设计环节做了阐释，将"合作"的概念引进课堂，打破传统的教学模式，为创设小组合作学习教学模式奠定了基础。但是，在高中英语语法课堂中构建有效的小组合作学习模式的策略，以及小组合作学习模式的具体实施步骤和方法仍需探索与完善。

综上所述，作为高中英语教师，我们在英语语法教学过程中和设计语法教学活动时也应重视合作学习模式的运用，如此既能促进学生合作能力的发展，又能确保良好的教学效果。

第三节　最近发展区理论

前苏联著名心理学家维果斯基（1896—1934）率先提出了最近发展区理论。该理论主要指学习者在不借助外力、独立解决问题时的水平与在他人帮助或指导下所能达到的解决问题的水平之间的差距。他认为，任何教育工作的开展均应基于学生的最近发展区，而教育所扮演的角色应当是赋予学生最近发展区经验，并切实培养学生的自主学习能力，如此方能切实推动学生综合学习能力的发展。随后，基于维果茨基的最近发展区理论，Berk.L&Winsler.A.在其所发表的研究报告中指出，教师应主动给予学生帮助，使其获得达到潜在发展水平的能力。当然，在此过程中，教师也不能一味地给予帮助，而是要让学生在经过指导之后，当其今后再遇到类似问题时，能在独立的情况下完成任务、解决问题。Burkit.E.则认为，教师的工作应是基于学生当前的学习水平逐步展开的，如此才能有助于学生思维能力的培养与发展。最初的最近发展区概念虽大多适用于研究儿童的心理发展，但随着研究的不断深入，该理论也逐渐成为许多后生理念的先导，如当前为世人所熟知的"支架"教学理念便是基于维果茨基所提出的最近发展区理论。"支架"教学的概念与最近发展区理论之间有异曲同工之妙，即指在教育领域中儿童从成人或同伴处获得帮助或引导来完成自己无法独立完成的任务。对此，国内外学者也进行了大量的实践与研究。如Morga.A.在经过研究后提出，"支架"应在学习者完成任务或获得独立解决问题的能力之后立即予以拆除，如此方能切实提升学生利用所学知识解决问题的能力。

基于最近发展区理论，教师在授课之前必须深入了解学生的学情，明确学生目前所处的学习阶段和水平，其授课内容的难易程度、教学进度的快慢节奏、教学活动的设置与安排都应该与学生已经具备的能力水平相吻合。教师要根据学生已有的知识水平因材施教，在学生学习的过程中给予足够的关注和适时的帮助与引导，突出教师的主导地位和学生的主体地位，再通过适时、恰当的教学评价来激发学生的创造性思维，使学生在学习的过程中保持持续的学习力，从而促使学生成功跨越最近发展区，实现潜在能力水平的突破。

具体到高中英语语法教学课堂，所谓的"支架"是指教师通过设置理解性和实践性的课堂活动，指导和帮助学生在感知、发现、体验和运用中获取新的语法知识。在学生初步获得新的语法知识之后，教师通过设置迁移创新类活动来促进学生巩固新知，进而逐步使学生原本的认知水平达到潜在的发展水平。

基于以上观点，作为高中英语教师，我们在设计课堂教学活动时，首先要了解学生当前的学习水平，唯有基于学生现有的学习水平，方能设计出最符合学生认知能力与规律的学习活动；其次要在设置学习任务时以激发学生学习兴趣为主；最后要在学生自主学习的过程中善于观察，通过提问以及引导的方式来减少学生的学习障碍，从而确保良好的课堂教学效果。

第四节　学习活动观理论

《普通高中英语课程标准（2017年版2020年修订）》中明确提出了指向学科核心素养发展的英语学习活动观，明确活动是英语学习的基本形式，是学习者学习和尝试运用语言理解与表达意义，培养文化意识，发展多元思维，形成学习能力的主要途径。学习活动观的提出为整合课程内容、实施深度教学、落实课程总目标提供了有力保障，也为变革学生的学习方式、提升英语教与学的效果提供了可操作的途径。教师应从英语学习活动观的视角重新审视课堂教学设计的合理性和有效性，整合课程内容，优化教学方式，为学生设计有情境、有层次、有实效的英语学习活动。

《普通高中英语课程标准（2017年版2020年修订）》还指出，英语学习活动的设计应以促进学生英语学科核心素养的发展为目标，围绕主题语境，基于口头和书面等多模态形式的语篇，通过学习理解、应用实践、迁移创新等层层递进的语言、思维、文化相融合的活动，引导学生加深对主题意义的理解；帮助学生在活动中习得语言知识，运用语言技能，阐释文化内涵，比较文化异同，评析语篇意义，形成正确的价值观和积极的情感态度，进而尝试在新的语境中运用所学语言和文化知识，分析问题、解决问题，创造性地表达个人观点、情感和态度。

具体而言，学习理解类活动主要包括感知与注意、获取与梳理、概括与整合等基于语篇的学习活动。例如，教师围绕主题创设情境，激活学生已有的知识和经验，铺垫必要的语言和文化背景知识，引出要解决的问题。在此基础上，以解决问题为目的，鼓励学生从语篇中获得新知，通过梳理、概括、整合信息，建立信息间的关联，形成新的知识结构，感知并理解语言所表达的意义和语篇所承载的文化价值取向。

应用实践类活动主要包括描述与阐释、分析与判断、内化与运用等深入语篇的学习活动，即在学习理解类活动的基础上，教师引导学生围绕主题和形成的新的知识结构开展描述、阐释、分析、判断等交流活动，逐步实现对语言知识和文化知识的内化，巩固新的知识结构，促进语言运用的自动化，助力学生将知识转化为能力。

迁移创新类活动主要包括推理与论证、批判与评价、想象与创造等超越语篇的学习活动，即教师引导学生针对语篇背后的价值取向或作者态度进行推理与论证，赏析语篇的文体特征与修辞手法，探讨其与主题意义的关联，批判、评价作者的观点等，加深对主题意义的理解，进而使学生在新的语境中，基于新的知识结构，通过自主、合作、探究的学习方式，综合运用语言技能，进行多元思维，创造性地解决陌生情境中的问题，理性表达观点、情感和态度，体现正确的价值观，实现深度学习，促进能力向素养的转化。

基于此，教师所设计的学习活动应该具备以下特征：①情境创设要尽量真实，注意与学生已有的知识和经验建立紧密联系，力求直接、简洁、有效；②教师要善于运用多种工具和手段，如思维导图或信息结构图，引导学生通过自主与合作相结合的方式，完成对信息的获取与梳理、概括与整合、内化与运用，教会学生在零散的信息和新旧知识之间建立关联，归纳和提炼基于主题的新知识结构；③教师要善于提出从理解到应用、从分析到评价等有层次的问题，引导学生的思维由低阶向高阶稳步发展，同时启发学生积极参与针对语篇内容和形式的讨论和反思，鼓励学生围绕有争议的话题有理有据地表达个人的情感与观点；④在情境创设中，教师要考虑地点、场合、交际对象、人物关系和交际目的等，提示学生有意识地根据语境选择恰当的语言形式，确保交际得体有效；⑤教师要根据所学主题内容、学习目标和学生经验等，选择和组织不同层次的英语学习活动。

因为学生在高中阶段所学习的英语语法知识是他们在初中阶段所学习的语法知识的延伸和发展，所以在高中英语语法课堂教学过程中，教师要努力设计具有综合性、关联性和实践性特点的英语学习活动，使学生通过学习理解、应用实践、迁移创新等一系列融语言知识、文化意识和思维品质为一体的活动，基于已有的知识，依托不同类型的语篇，在分析问题和解决问题的过程中，促进自身语言知识学习、语言技能发展、文化内涵理解、多元思维发展、价值取向判断和学习策略运用。这一过程既是语言知识与语言技能整合发展的过程，也是文化意识不断增强、思维品质不断提升、学习能力不断提高的过程。目前，我国正在全面推进新课程改革，如何采用科学、有效的教学方法来激发学生学习英语的主动性和自觉性，最终提高学生的语言综合运用能力，已成为每一位英语教师面临的重要课题。

第五节　深度学习理论

深度学习（Deep Learning）是美国学者Ference Marton和Roger Saljo在1976年基于大学生文本阅读学习结果的研究中提出的概念。在我国，关于深度学习的研究起步较晚。2005年，黎加厚教授在《促进学生深度学习》这一著作中最早提出深度学习概念。此后，深度学习概念走入我国研究者的视野，但发展缓慢。直至2017年，深度学习成为国内研究者的一个热门研究话题，但主要集中于计算机软件及计算机应用、自动化技术领域。教育理论和教育管理领域对深度学习也开始有所关注。2020年7月，上海师范大学教育学院副教授、学习共同体研究学院院长陈静静博士出版了《学习共同体——走向深度学习》一书，把深度学习与学科学习再次紧密相连，并在教育理论和教学管理领域掀起了巨大的波澜，她也因此成为国内深度学习与学科学习研究方面的领军人物。

陈静静博士认为学生在学习过程中走向深度学习的有效途径是构建学习共同体。那么，什么是学习共同体呢？实际上，学习共同体这一教育模式最早是由美国教育家杜威提出来的。日本东京大学佐藤学教授将学习共同体构想引入自己的教育改革实践中。他提出学习共同体就是要使学校成为儿童合作学习的场所，成为教师相互学习的场所，成为家长与市民参与学校教育并相互学习的场所。我们可以这样来理解：学习共同体是为了更好地学习而形成的相互联系的整体，意味着学生之间、教师之间、学校之间、家长之间的密切协作和相互学习，其共同目标是为每个学生提供高品质的学习机会，其两个核心理念是平等和倾听。学习共同体的课堂本质上是建立温暖和谐、平等互助的人际关系，让学生在这种轻松、自主和协同的学习氛围中自由表达自己的观点，同时倾听同伴的观点，从而实现资源共享，在倾听和切磋中成长，也只有这样学生的课堂学习才会真实地发生，才可能有一定的深度，从而促进学生学习素养的形成与发展。因此，陈静静博士认为学生的课堂学习要想真实地发生，一般需要具备六个必要条件（6s），即学生具有充分的心理安全（safety），学习内容对学生具有重要的意义和价值（significance），学生体会到自己在学习中的主体作用（subjectivities），学习内容具有挑战性（struggling），学习时间比较充分（sufficient），学习过程中有必要的人际支持（support）。学生只有在相互信任、相互倾听、和谐友好等自在平等的学习氛围中，才能感受到真正的轻松、无压力，才能够放心舒适地说出自己在学习中遇到的问题和困惑，并能得到同伴的帮助。同时，在学生学习的过程中，教师应该安排具有一定难度和挑战性的教学内容，并给予学生足够的学习时间，通过激发学生的学习积极性，充分调动其学习主体的意识，如此才能将学习从浅表推向深入，学生的思维也才能从低阶向高阶迈进。

如何让学生的学习在英语语法课堂中真实地发生，让那些不爱学习语法的学生重新进入自主、合作的学习状态，让那些只追求学习成绩和应付学习任务的学生更加自主、持久地深度学习呢？基于对陈静静博士和她的学习共同体领航教师们的大量课堂观察和课例研究，教师应该从学生的口语表达和书面习作中收集出错案例，通过准确把握学生的学习需求，结合目标语法特点和学生的学习特点，设计出少而精的学习单和与学生生活实际相关的课堂活动链，为学生相互学习、相互倾听创造空间和平台，从而使学生有兴趣、持续、积极地参与到课堂学习中来，以达到提升课堂品质的目的。

下 篇
教学实践

依据《普通高中英语课程标准（2017年版2020年修订）》中对语法知识内容以及教学提示的要求，本书中的语法教学实践设计均是在英语学习活动观的指导下，根据语法项目选用恰当的主题语境，并根据主题语境设置学习理解、应用实践、迁移创新类活动，让学生在自主、合作式学习中通过感受、体验、领悟、交流、展示等相关学习行为不断加深对语法项目的理解，并通过完成相关的家庭作业进行语法知识的巩固和内化。通过对主题语境、教学目标、教学过程的综述，读者能够对本书中英语学习活动观指导下的语法教学实践设计有一个更加清晰的了解，从而更加深刻地感受英语学习活动观对英语教学的深刻影响和指导意义。

第一章

定语从句教学设计

第一节 that，which，who，whose
引导的定语从句

教学设计一——城市介绍

Step 1. Lead-in：A guessing game.

1. It is a city that/which is close to Beijing and Tianjin.

2. The people who want to make a trip to the city can enjoy Ping Opera（评剧）.

3. It is a city whose nickname is Northern Porcelain Capital（北方瓷都）.

4. The city which/that was destroyed by a big earthquake in 1976 takes on a new look now.

【Design intention】A guessing game is used to introduce the teaching target in this class and arouse students' interest as well.

Step 2. Read the following dialogue and try to answer the questions using attributive clauses.

The Guide：Welcome to Tangshan. Honored to be your guide，I'll spare no efforts to answer you any question concerning this city.

Tourist A: So would you please give us a brief introduction about Tangshan?

The Guide: Well, it is a costal city, located in the northeast of Hebei, and close to Beijing and Tianjin.

Tourist B: What is it famous for?

The Guide: It is well-known for Ping Opera and Shadow Play（皮影）. Tourists making a trip here can appreciate these local dramas well. Plus, bone china（骨瓷）native to Tangshan enjoys great fame at home and abroad. So Tangshan is also called Northern Porcelain Capital by many people.

Tourist C: Wow! That sounds great. And I've heard that Tangshan was once destroyed by a big earthquake. What about its current situation?

The Guide: Yes, the city was destroyed by a big earthquake in 1976, but it takes on a new look now.

Tourists: Thank you for your sharing.

The Guide: My pleasure. Hope you can enjoy yourselves here.

【Design intention】In this part, students will have a rough understanding of the attributive clauses introduced by that/which/who/whose by reading and experiencing the paraphrasing sentences.

Questions:

1. Where is Tangshan?

Tangshan is a coastal city that/which is located in the northeast of Hebei, close to Beijing and Tianjin.

2. Who can enjoy Ping Opera and Shadow Play（皮影）?

Tourists who make a trip to Tangshan can enjoy Ping Opera and Shadow Play（皮影）.

3. What is Tangshan's nickname?

Tangshan, famous for bone china（骨瓷）, is a modern industrial city whose nickname is Northern Porcelain Capital.

4. What happened to Tangshan in 1976?

Tangshan which was destroyed by a big earthquake in 1976 takes on a new look now.

Step 3. Practice：Make riddles and play a guessing game in the class.

Activity 1. Work in groups to make riddles according to the given information in the envelop.

① Beijing：

   ◆ a long history

   ◆ very cold and dry winter

   ◆ attract many visitors from home and abroad every year

   ◆ a fast pace of life

   ◆ the capital of China

② Shanghai：

   ※ lie in the east of China

   ※ an international city

   ※ people, sweet food such as dessert

   ※ world-famous for its fast economic development

   ※ Oriental Pearl TV Tower

③ Xi'an：

   ● warm-hearted people

   ● convenient transport

   ● home to a lot of historical sites

   ● located in the middle of the Guanzhong Plain

   ● used as the capital of 13 dynasties

④ Chongqing：

   ☆ a long history

   ☆ rich in tourism resources

   ☆ one of the hottest cities in China

   ☆ spicy food such as hotpot

   ☆ nickname— "a mountain city"

⑤ Hangzhou：

   ▲ the capital city

   ▲ lie to the south of the Changjiang River

▲ famous for its beautiful scenery

▲ home to the Longjing Tea

▲ nickname— "Heaven on Earth"

⑥ Harbin：

★ the capital city

★ lie in the northern part of China

★ cold and long winter

★ famous for all kinds of winter activities

★ nickname— "Ice City"

Requirements：

1. The student who describes the city is expected to use the attributive clauses including that，which，who and whose（at least 3 sentences）．

2. The student who tells the riddles should give the information about the city sentence by sentence，trying not to let others get the answer directly.

Example：

It is a city that has a long history.

The people who live there have a fast pace of life.

It is a city whose winter is very cold and dry.

The city which attracts many visitors from home and abroad every year is the capital of China.

Activity 2. Play a guessing game in the class.

Every group leader speaks out their riddles and others will guess what city it is.

Attention：

The student who guesses the riddle should not only give the answer but tell the reasons as well.

Example：

It's Tangshan because Tangshan is a city which/that was destroyed by a big earthquake in 1976.

【Design intention】By making riddles and guessing games，students will be provided opportunities to learn to use the attributive clauses effectively in an open and happy atmosphere. At the same time, they are encouraged to take an active part in the activities.

Step **4**. Writing.

Supposing your pen pal Lucy wants to travel to China, she hopes you can recommend her a city to visit. Please choose one city above to recommend and try to explain the reasons.

Attention：

1. Please try to use attributive clauses as many as possible.

2. Every correct attributive clause is worth 10 points.

【Design intention】The purpose of this writing is to give the students another chance to help them consolidate what they have learned in this class and at the same time arouse their cultural confidence and national pride, namely "using English to tell stories of our Chinese". Of course, their creative thinking will be developed.

Step **5**. Presentation.

Two or three students are invited to share the city that they would like to recommend to Lucy with their classmates.

Step **6**. Homework.

1. Polish your recommendation if you make some mistakes.

2. You can also choose another city to recommend to Lucy and try to use as many attributive clauses introduced by that, which, who and whose as possible.

教学设计二——影视赏析

Step **1**. Lead-in：Enjoy a video（*Looking Up*）.

1. *Looking up* is a touching movie which/that attracts lots of viewers.

2. The boy is Ma Fei who/that used to be a poor performer at school.

3. Ma Fei whose father used to be a bridge designer finally became an astronaut.

【Design intention】A brief introduction of the film is used to introduce the teaching target in this class and arouse students' interest as well.

Step 2. Observe and summarize.

1. *Looking Up* is a touching movie. The movie attracts lots of viewers.

→ *Looking Up* is a touching moving which/that attracts lots of viewers.

2. The boy is Ma Fei. The boy used to be a poor performer at school.

→ The boy is Ma Fei who/that used to be a poor performer at school.

3. Ma Fei's father used to be a bridge designer. Ma Fei finally became an astronaut.

→ Ma Fei whose father used to be a bridge designer finally became an astronaut.

【Design intention】In this part, students will have a basic understanding of the attributive clauses introduced by that/which/who/whose through observation and discovery, and then they will have the ability to conclude basic rules of the attributive clauses.

Step 3. Practice: Combine the two sentences into one by using the attributive clauses.

Activity 1. Work in groups to make up sentences.

1. *Looking up* tells us a touching story.

The story is about love and family affection.

2. This man is called Ma Haowen.

This man was cheated by his friend and put in prison for 7 years.

3. Ma Haowen was released and started a new life with his son.

His son became less interested in studying.

4. Mr. Yan is a strict director at school.

Mr. Yan decides to remove Ma Fei from school.

5. Ma Fei was faced with huge pressure.

The pressure came from the school.

6. The bet finally came true.

His father made a bet with Mr. Yan.

Activity 2. Presentation.

Each group leader shares the sentences in his/her group with the whole class.

1. *Looking Up* tells us a touching story which/that is about love and family affection.

2. This man who/that was cheated by his friend and put in prison for 7 years is called Ma Haowen.

3. Ma Haowen was released and started a new life with his son who/that became less interested in studying.

4. Mr. Yan who/that decides to remove Ma Fei from school is a strict director at school.

5. Ma Fei was faced with huge pressure which/that came from the school.

6. The bet which/that his father made with Mr. Yan finally came true.

【Design intention】By making up sentences related to the plot of the movie, students will be easily aroused to learn to use the attributive clauses effectively. At the same time they are encouraged to take an active part in the activities.

Step 4. Writing.

Rewrite the end of the story by changing the underlined sentences into attributive clauses.

Miss Gao also helped Ma Fei a lot. She is his head teacher. In his special education way, Ma Haowen taught his son not only the knowledge, but also the courage and confidence. The courage and confidence made Ma Fei become the top student in school. It surprised Mr. Yan. He is the school director. He didn't regard Ma Fei as a bad boy any longer. At last, Ma Fei ended up as an astronaut.

In this film, we see a great father, Ma Haowen. He gives his son enough love and trust. The love and trust pave the way for Ma Fei's success. It also gives a good lesson for those parents. Those parents only care about children's grades. As parents, we should pay more attention to children's mental health than grades and spend more time with our children. Because love and care are what they need most.

【Design intention】The purpose of this writing is to give the students another chance to help them consolidate what they have learned in this class, and at the same time arouse their reflection on the relationship with their parents and great paternal love.

Step **5**. Presentation.

Two students will be asked to share their continuation of the story and others try to help make corrections.

Step **6**. Homework.

Write a film review of *Looking Up* and try to use what you have learned in this class.

教学设计三——文化遗产

Step **1**. Warming-up：Enjoy a short video（*National Treasure*）.

National Treasure is a TV show which is designed to introduce the Chinese traditional culture by telling the story of the cultural relics.

【Design intention】The video is used to introduce the theme of the class and arouse students' interest as well.

Step **2**. Lead-in：A guessing game.

1. It is a vase which/that is painted with blue and white.

2. The people who cherish it want to see it in the museum.

3. There is a song whose name is the same as the vase.

4. It is a cultural relic which represents the typical artifact of porcelain（瓷器）in China.

【Design intention】In this part, students can perceive the basic structure of the attributive clauses introduced by that/which/who/whose. Besides, it also can encourage students to take an active part in this part.

Step **3**. Observe and summarize.

1. It is a vase which/that is painted with blue and white.

⟶ It is a vase. The vase is painted with blue and white.

2. The people who cherish it want to see it in the museum.

⟶ The people want to see it in the museum. The people cherish it.

3. There is a song whose name is the same as the vase.

⟶ There is a song. The song's name is the same as the vase.

4. It is a cultural relic <u>which</u> represents the typical artifact of porcelain in China.

⟶ It is a cultural relic. The cultural relic represents the typical artifact of porcelain in China.

【Design intention】In this part, students need to divide each sentence into two parts, which can help them to understand the basic usage of the antecedent and the function of each relative pronouns. Then they will have the ability to conclude basic rules of the attributive clauses.

Step 4. Practice：Role-play.

Supposing now you are a tour guide, you need to choose one of the cultural relics to introduce it to the foreigners.

Activity 1. The students work in groups to discuss how to introduce the cultural relics by using the given information.

Terracotta Army：

1. A huge army of life-size warriors and horses

2. Buried with the remains of the First Emperor

3. One of the eight wonders in the world

4. Colorfully painted and vivid

5. Located in Xi'an

Paper-cutting：

1. Non-material cultural heritage

2. A special folk art（民间艺术）

3. A history of nearly 1,000 years

4. Window-covering

5. Popular in many areas

Shadow play（皮影戏）：

1. A form of drama

2. The world's earliest "movie art"

3. A history of more than 2,000 years

4. People use five bamboo sticks to act

5. Performers stand behind a white screen

Marquis Yi chime bells（曾侯乙编钟）：

1. A kind of musical instrument

2. Consist of 65 bells arranged in three rows

3. In different shape and size

4. Need five musicians to play

5. Produce all the tones of a modern piano

Requirement：

The students who describe the cultural relics need to use attributive clauses as many as possible.

Activity 2. Introduce the cultural relics in the class.

Every group leader speaks out their introduction and others will give some comments. The group which introduces the relic most clearly and vividly will be recognized as the champion.

【Design intention】By using the given information to introduce the cultural relics, students will be provided opportunities to master the usage of the attributive clauses effectively. In addition, an active atmosphere will be created to encourage students to express their ideas freely. What's more, students' cultural awareness will be improved.

Step 5. Writing.

Supposing you are going to serve as a volunteer in a museum to introduce the cultural relics to the foreigners, the visitors hope you can introduce one of the treasures for better understanding. Please choose one cultural relic above to introduce and try to explain the reasons.

Tips：

Please try to use attributive clauses as many as possible.

【Design intention】The writing activity is used to help students consolidate what they have learned today. Meanwhile, it can arouse students' national pride.

Step 6. Presentation.

Two or three students share their introduction of the cultural relics in the class and others try to make comments on the presented writing.

Step 7. Homework.

1. Polish your introduction according to the comments given by your classmates and teacher if it is not good enough.

2. You can also challenge yourself to choose another cultural relic you have known to introduce and try to use attributive clauses as many as possible.

教学设计四——西藏之旅

Step 1. Lead-in：A guessing game.

In August，Remi decided to start her self-driving trip to Tibet. She organized some information about the place of departure.

1. It is a city. The city is located in the middle of the Guanzhong Plain.

⟶ It is a city that/which is located in the middle of the Guanzhong Plain.

2. People love Chinese history. People have a special feeling for the city.

⟶ People who/that love Chinese history have a special feeling for the city.

3. The city was the capital of 13 dynasties. The city is the capital of Shannxi province now.

⟶ The city which/that was the capital of 13 dynasties is the capital of Shannxi province now.

【Design intention】In this part，students are expected to guess the name of the city，Xi'an，the first station of Remi's trip according to the given sentences，which aims to stimulate students' passion and introduce the target grammar in this class.

Step 2. The Land of Abundance—Chengdu.

Setting off from Xi'an，Remi decided to get into Tibet from Sichuan. So after a long day's driving，she arrived in Chengdu.

Chengdu which/that is the capital city of Sichuan Province is located in Chengdu Plain. It is a city whose nickname is "the Land of Abundance". People who/that live in Chengdu seem to lead a cosy life with less pressure. The pace of life in Chengdu is slower than that in other big cities. Remi went to many famous streets <u>whose</u> features are various snacks. Not only did she play with the cute panda <u>that/which</u> is regarded as the national treasure but she also enjoyed shopping in the most famous place whose name is Taikoo Li. Chengdu is really a city <u>that/which</u> one wants to come to but doesn't want to leave from.

【Design intention】Step 2 is the second station of Remi's trip. In this short passage, there are many attributive clauses introduced by that, which, who and whose. From these sentences, students can experience the basic rules of the attributive clauses. And also, from the storyline, students will know more about Remi's trip to Tibet, and know more about our beautiful country. So from step1 to step 2, it is not only a process from the use of the grammar knowledge in sentences to a passage but a process of Remi's travel, and the two benefit the students to better understand the target grammar.

Step 3. Organize the information.

After a short stay in Chengdu, Remi drove to Ya'an. The following is some information about Ya'an.

Location:

1. located in the Sichuan—Tibet, Sichuan and Yunnan Road intersection

2. 120 kilometers away from Chengdu

3. "the Throat of West Sichuan" and "the Gateway to Tibet"

Culture:

1. a historical and cultural city in Sichuan Province

2. the birthplace of tea culture

3. the habitat of the giant panda in Sichuan

History:

1. destroyed by a big earthquake in 2013

2. many well-preserved cultural relics of the Han Dynasty

3. the origin of "the Tea Horse Ancient Road"

Requirements:

1. Use attributive clauses introduced by that, which, who and whose as many

as possible.

2. Every correct attributive clause is worth 10 points.

Example：

1. Ya'an is a city which/that is the habitat of the giant panda in Sichuan.

2. Ya'an whose nickname is "the Throat of West Sichuan" is located in the Sichuan—Tibet, Sichuan and Yunnan Road intersection.

【Design intention】In the previous two steps, students have got some information about Xi'an and Chengdu, and they already have had the interest to continue the trip to Tibet. Besides, much information about Xi'an and Chengdu is expressed by using attributive clauses, which helps students get the grammar knowledge. So it is time for them to organize the information about Ya'an by using what they have learned.

Step **4.** Persuade your friend.

Remi didn't want to travel alone, and she wanted to persuade her friend Amy to travel together. So she wrote a letter to Amy at that time. We don't know what she wrote, but if you were Remi, what would you write?

Reference：

Idea 1：Tell Amy what she experienced.

● Xi'an（Remi left from Xi'an）

● Chengdu & Ya'an（Remi got into Tibet from Chengdu by way of Ya'an）

Idea 2：Tell Amy what she will experience in the rest of the journey.

● Sights：Xinduqiao town（ "Photo Paradise" ）

Daocheng Yading（ alien landforms ）

Tips:

1. You can use what you have learned to tell Amy what Remi experienced according to the idea 1.

2. If you want to challenge more, the idea 2 will be a good choice. You can add some reasonable imagination according to the given information to tell Amy what Remi will experience.

3. That the idea 1 and the idea 2 are combined is allowed.

Requirements:

1. You are expected to use attributive clauses including that, which, who and whose.

2. Every correct attributive clause is worth 10 points.

3. Each group is expected to have at least three attributive clauses.

Example:

Idea 1:

Dear Amy,

My trip to Tibet has begun and I am writing to invite you to travel with me. I set off from Xi'an and now I am at Ya'an. Xi'an is a city that/which is located in the middle of the Guanzhong Plain. The city which/that was the capital of 13 dynasties is the capital city of Shannxi province now. The city leaves a special impression on me. Do you know Chengdu whose nickname is "the Land of Abundance"? After a long day's driving from Xi'an, I arrived in Chengdu. It is a city which/that is home to the panda. I played with pandas who are so cute. There are bound to be more and more interesting things along the journey, so I hope you can join me!

Yours,

Remi

Idea 2:

Dear Amy,

How is everything going with you? I remember that you are always longing to travel to Tibet. And my trip there has started and I'm writing to invite you to join me. I left Xi'an and arrived at Ya'an now. I am going to set off from Ya'an whose nickname is "the Throat of West Sichuan" to Daocheng Yading by way of Xinduqiao. Today, I looked up some information about the two places on the Internet. Xinduqiao is a place whose nickname is "Photo Paradise". It is a place which is known for the beautiful grassland and rolling mountains. I hope you can join me to experience more wonderful things along the coming journey!

Yours,

Remi

【Design intention】From step 3 to step 4, it is actually an exercise from sentence making to passage writing. In step 4, two different ideas are given, and actually they have different levels of difficulty, which will encourage the students of different levels to challenge. In previous steps, students have got some information about Xi'an, Chengdu and Ya'an, so the idea 1 is provided, which is easier. Meanwhile, some students may want to challenge more, so the idea 2 is provided, they can use the grammar knowledge that they have learned to describe the new places that they have not known.

Step 5. Share your letter.

Two students share their letters and others try to help them make the letters better.

Step 6. Homework.

Is your letter persuasive? If not, try to polish your reasons to persuade Amy to join you and be sure to use as many attributive clauses as possible.

第二节 where，when，why引导的定语从句

教学设计一——亲子关系

Step 1. Lead-in：Guess who she is.

1. She is someone who will selflessly do millions of chores for you.

2. She is someone who will eventually get old as you grow up.

3. She is someone who will burst into tears for your happiness and sadness.

4. She is someone whose heart is completely filled with your growth.

5. She is someone whose eyes are perpetually fixed on your change.

6. She is someone who is the right person we are grateful to.

【Design intention】A guessing game is used to review the attributive clauses introduced by relative pronouns and arouse students' interest as well. Moreover, it is used to lead in the teaching target of this class.

Step 2. Pair work：Work in pairs to ask and answer the following questions.

1. Do you remember the first time when you saw your mother cry or smile?

2. Can you describe the place where the above scene happened?

3. What's the reason why your mother cried or smiled?

4. What's your feeling about the occasion when you saw your mother cry or smile?

【Design intention】Through observing and answering the questions, students will have a basic understanding of the attributive clauses introduced by when/where/why. During this period, students are encouraged to find out the answers using attributive clauses introduced by when/where/why as well.

Step 3. Fill in blanks and do a role-play.

Activity 1. Work in groups to fill in the blanks to complete the dialogue.

（Supposing the Mother's Day is approaching, student 1 is the host and student 2 is invited to share an unforgettable scene where he/she saw his/her mother cry or smile.)

S1: Good day to you! Welcome to our School News Center _____ all the historical events are documented. Next Monday is Mother's Day _____ all of us will express our gratitude to our mothers. So can you share the most impressive scene happening to you and your mother?

S2: Yes, I'd love to. I still remember the first time _____ I saw my mother cry. It was the street _____ all the passers-by just paid attention to themselves. Suddenly, we were separated by the crowd.

S1: What happened next?

S2: 20 minutes later, I saw my mother crying overwhelmingly. The time we hugged each other is the most precious memory. On some occasions _____ I've gone through ups and downs, I will talk with her. I don't know the reason _____ I rely on her so much.

S1: Maybe she is the person _____ is right there waiting for you.

S2: You are right. On this special day, I'd like to say "thank you" to my dear mother. The reason _____ I am grateful to her is that she is always offering me the unconditional love.

S1: Thank you for your sharing. Remember to express your gratitude to your mother.

Activity 2. Do the role-play.

（Each group is required to do the role-play. If necessary, students are encouraged to make up a new one. ）

Attention:

The students who make up a new one should use the attributive clauses introduced by when/where/why.

【Design intention】Through filling in the blanks, students will be provided the related context to learn the usages of relative adverbs when/where/why effectively. At the same time they are inspired to recall the impressive scene about their mothers, thus arousing their emotion to express their gratitude.

Step 4. Reading and filling.

Having listened to dialogue from the News Center, the mother herself wrote a letter to her son.

Dear son,

Enormously touched by your words, I also remember the scene _____ I lost sight of your figure. I will never forget the time _____ I saw your face. Actually, listening to the news, I recalled the occasion _____ I read the book written by Long Yingtai. As Long says, "Parent-child relationship means that you stand on the side of the road _____ parents eyewitness children's figures gradually disappear in silence and never chase forward." However, I still hope that I can accompany you whenever needed.

So moved am I that I can't wait to express myself. It was more than ten years ___ _____ you and I explore the newly-built world _____ both of us seek the balance of parentage. Simultaneously, the reason _____ I'd like to express myself is that you unfold the world full of beauty and sincerity. Though we have gone through some occasions _____ we are faced with disagreement, I still treasure the past time we spent together and expect the future world _____ we better understand each other.

In a nutshell, I cherish any case _____ we have experienced joy and sorrow together. Thank you, my dear son. My true emotion/gratitude is beyond the words.

Yours,

Mom

【Design intention】The purpose of filling in the blanks is to help students consolidate what they have learned in this class. Meanwhile, reading this letter enables students to arouse their inner emotion for maternal love, namely "using English to express what we want to convey to others". At the same time, students are motivated to know how to write a letter of thanks, which can pave the way for their writing.

Step 5. Writing.

Supposing the Mother's Day is coming, our School News Center is collecting letters of thanks. Please write a letter to your mother and try to show the reasons.

Attention:

1. Please try to use attributive clauses introduced by when/where/why as many as possible.

2. Every correct attributive clause is worth 10 points.

【Design intention】This part is designed to aid students to put what they have learned into practical use. Meanwhile, students are expected to express themselves in English correctly by using the grammar, which is indispensable for them to form an English thinking mode and understand the difference between Chinese and English better.

Step 6. Presentation.

Two students are invited to share their letters of thanks and others try to make a correction and give a point they deserve.

【Design intention】In this part, for the students, they will get a chance to improve each other. They can improve themselves by correcting others, which is a good way for them to have a deep understanding about what they have learned. For the teacher, it is more conductive to judge the students harvest in this class.

Step 7. Homework.

1. Polish your letter of thanks according to the comments from your classmates and teacher.

2. Read your letter to your mom.

教学设计二——传统节日

Step 1. Lead-in: A guessing game.

1. It is one of the most important festivals in China when we will wear new clothes and get together with our family members to enjoy the meals, including dumplings.

2. Children will receive the red envelops where the lucky money is kept.

3. The reason why we celebrate this festival is to welcome the coming of the new

year.

【Design intention】A guessing game is used to introduce the teaching target in this class and arouse students' interest as well.

Step 2. Read and summarize.

1. It is one of the most important festivals in China.

During the festival, we will wear new clothes and get together with our family members to enjoy the meals, including dumplings.

⟶ It is one of the most important festivals in China when we will wear new clothes and get together with our family members to enjoy the meals, including dumplings.

2. Children will receive the red envelops.

The lucky money is kept in the red envelops.

⟶ Children will receive the red envelops where the lucky money is kept.

3. The reason is to welcome the coming of the new year.

We celebrate this festival for it.

⟶ The reason why we celebrate this festival is to welcome the coming of the new year.

4. It is a festival.

We will enjoy watching the boat-racing game and eating Zongzi in the festival.

⟶ It is a festival when we will enjoy watching the boat-racing game and eating Zongzi.

5. The reason is that we want to admire an ancient poet Qu Yuan.

We celebrate the festival for it.

⟶ The reason why we celebrate the festival is that we want to admire an ancient poet Qu Yuan.

6. People will hold the boat-racing game in the Mi Luo river.

Qu Yuan drawned himself in the river.

⟶ People will hold the boat-racing game in the Mi Luo river where Quan drawned himself.

Summary：

It is one of the most important festivals in China _____ we will wear new clothes and get together with our family members to enjoy the meals，including dumplings.

Children will receive the red envelops _____ the lucky money is kept.

The reason _____ we celebrate this festival is to welcome the coming of the new year.

It is a festival _____ we will enjoy watching the boat-racing game and eating Zongzi.

The reason _____ we celebrate the festival is that we want to admire an ancient poet Qu Yuan.

People will hold the boat-racing game in the Mi Luo river _____ Quan drawned himself.

【Design intention】In this part，students will have a basic understanding of the attributive clauses introduced by when/where/why through observation and discovery, and then they will have the ability to conclude basic rules of attributive clauses.

Step 3. Practice：Make riddles and play a guessing game in the class.

Activity 1. Work in groups to make riddles according to the given information in the envelop.

Mid-autumn festival：

◆ enjoy mooncakes

◆ get together with family members

◆ admire the moon

Double Nine festival：

※ visit and care about the old people

※ climb the mountain

※ arouse people's awareness of caring about the old

Tomb-sweeping day/Qing Ming festival：

● clean tombs

● light incenses and bring paper-cutting flowers to the dead

● honor the dead

● show our respect to our ancestors

Qi Qiao festival：

☆ meet Zhi Nv once a year

☆ show best wishes to unmarried girls

☆ show love for beloved ones

Zhong Yuan festival：

▲ honor our ancestors

▲ wish the ancestors to rest in peace

▲ pray for blessings from our ancestors

Lantern festival：

★ hang the red lanterns in front of our houses

★ eat yuanxiao/tangyuan

★ get together with family members

★ celebrate the last day of the Spring Festival

Requirements：

1. The students who describe the festival must use attributive clauses including when, where and why.

2. The students who tell the riddles should give the information about the festivals sentence by sentence, trying not to let others get the answer directly.

Example：

It is a festival when we get together at night to have a feast.

We will watch the Spring Festival Gala where there are many fantastic programs.

The reason why we celebrated it in ancient times was to drive away the monster—Nian.

Activity 2. Play a guessing game in the class.

Every group leader speaks out their riddles, not only gives the answers but also tells the reason.

Example:

It's Spring Festival Eve because it is a festival when we will get together to enjoy the delicious dinner and watch the Spring Festival Gala in the evening.

【Design intention】By making riddles and guessing games, students will be provided opportunities to learn attributive clauses effectively in an open and happy atmosphere. At the same time, they are encouraged to take an active part in the activities. "Practice makes perfect." Therefore, through practice, students can better understand how to use the attributive clauses introduced by when, where and why.

Step 4. Writing.

Suppose your pen pal Lily is very interested in Chinese traditional festivals. and she hopes you can introduce one traditional festival to her. Please choose one festival above and introduce it to her so as to invite her to China to celebrate it with your family.

Attention:

1. Please try to use attributive clauses as many as possible.

2. Every correct attributive clause is worth 10 points.

【Design intention】The purpose of this writing is to give the students another chance to help them consolidate what they have learned in this class, at the same time arouse their cultural awareness and national pride, namely "using English to tell stories of our Chinese". Of course, their creative thinking will be developed during their writing.

Step 5. Presentation.

Two students will share their festivals in front of the class and others try to make some comments.

Step 6. Homework.

1. Is there any mistake in your description of the traditional festival? If any, polish it.

2. You can also choose another traditional festival to introduce and try to make more foreigners interested in it.

教学设计三——大众健康

Step 1. Lead-in：Watch a video.

Please watch a video about COVID-19 and answer the following three questions.

T：Hi，guys. Do you remember the time when COVID-19 broke out ?

Ss：The time _____ was in February 2020.

T：Can you tell me the place where COVID-19 took place first?

Ss：The place _____ first was not clear.

T：Do you know the reason why COVID-19 appeared suddenly in the world?

Ss：The reason _____ was still unknown.

【Design intention】Watching a video is aimed to arouse students' interest in this class，and the activity of ask-and-answer is designed to lead students to use the attributive clauses introduced by when，where and why. That is the target grammar in this class.

Step 2. Group work：Deliver a speech.

Supposing you are the spokesman of WHO，you are required to deliver a brief speech about the outbreak of COVID-19 in Wuhan including the time，the place and the reason.

Good morning! Regretting to tell you that the terrible virus has spread worldwide，I，as the spokesman of WHO，shoulder the responsibility to release the latest news to you. The time _____.

The place _____.

The reason _____.

Hope that people throughout the world carefully protect themselves.

【Design intention】In this part，students will have the chance to practice the attributive clauses introduced by when，where and why, and will have a basic understanding of the attributive clauses as well.

Step 3. An interview and a report.

Activity 1. If you are a reporter assigned to interview the spokesman of WHO, please complete the dialogue.

Reporter: Mr. Tedros, thank you for your speech about the epidemic. May I ask you several questions?

Spokesman: Sure.

Reporter: Can you tell us the time when WHO paid attention to it?

Spokesman: The time was in January, 2020.

Reporter: Could you please explain the reason why people should wear masks?

Spokesman: The reason _____ was that masks can help protect people from being infected.

Reporter: Do you know the exact place where the virus was found?

Spokesman: The place _____ is not proved.

Activity 2. Supposing you are the reporter, please narrate your interview to the public.

Requirement:

Try your best to use the attributive clauses introduced by when, where and why.

Example:

Good afternoon, everyone. I'm honored to interview the spokesman of WHO. The following is what he has referred to. To begin with, _____. In addition, _____. In the end, _____.

Hope everyone of us takes it seriously and fights it bravely.

【Design intention】 Through an interview and a report, students will be provided opportunities to learn to use the attributive clauses effectively in an open atmosphere. At the same time, they are encouraged to care about the big events around them and develop their social responsibility.

Step 4. Make a detailed report.

Supposing the chief-editor arranges for you to compose a detailed report related to the situation in Wuhan, please try your best to make it up by using the attributive clauses introduced by when, where and why.

Good afternoon, everyone. It is widely known that the outbreak of COVID-19 has threatened our health. It's my duty to tell you the details objectively. My report is made up of two parts. The former part comes from the speech of the spokesman of WHO. The details are as follows, _____.

The latter part is adapted from the interview of the spokesman of WHO. The relevant information can be summarized as follows, _____.

Nothing is more important than health. Please take care of yourselves deliberately.

【Design intention】The purpose of this part is to provide the students with another chance to help them consolidate what they have learned in this class, and at the same time arouse their interest in caring about the big events around them.

Step 5. Presentation.

Two students are invited to share their reports and others try to make some comments to help them make the reports better.

Step 6. Homework.

If you are invited to make a report about the outbreak of the epidemic of your hometown, please try your best to use the attributive clauses introduced by when, where and why.

教学设计四——成人仪式

Step 1. Lead-in: The activity before the class.

Dear teachers and students, welcome to the coming-of-age ceremony. Do you know the reason why we hold the ceremony? Let's enjoy the ceremony together.

【Design intention】Use the coming-of-age as the lead-in to arouse students' interest.

Step 2. The activities during the class.

Activity 1. Listen, fill and answer.

Welcome to be on the spot, dear teachers and students, respectable parents and guests. Today we will launch the coming-of-age ceremony. The reason _____ we choose today is that it is related to the Youth Day, _____ the hopeful and promising teenagers set foot on the coming adulthood. Although the situation _____ the Communist Party of China marked May 4th as a milestone in history was different from today, we still need the ceremony _____ it shows that teenagers are supposed to shoulder the responsibility to be qualified citizens and irreplaceable figures.

【Design intention】The purpose of listening to the clip is to introduce the teaching target—the attributive clauses introduced by when, where and why in this class. Students are expected to fill in the blanks with when, where and why introducing the attributive clauses.

Pair work: Work in pairs to ask and answer the following questions.

1. Why do we choose May 4th to hold the ceremony?

2. What's the information about the Youth Day?

3. Why do we still need the ceremony?

【Design intention】Through observing and answering the questions, students will have a basic understanding of attributive clauses introduced by when, where and why. During this stage, students are encouraged to be familiar with the structure as well.

Activity 2. Read and fill.

Read the speech delivered by a parent and fill in the blanks in groups.

Good afternoon, dear kids and teachers. Honored to share my feelings with you together, I am overwhelmingly stuck in this coming-of-age ceremony.

I will never forget the day _____ I accompanied my daughter three years ago. Just like my child, you are not what you used to be. You are walking on the path _____ you are supposed to think critically and behave reasonably. At this moment, I feel tremendously thrilled. The reason _____ I have that kind of feeling is that my dear daughter, like all of you, is experiencing psychological maturity.

Time and tide wait for no man. Hope you can cherish the precious time to become those who you want to be. I, like most parents, will be there whenever you need me, my dear kid.

【Design intention】By filling in the blanks, students will get familiar with relative words when, where and why. Involved in the activity, students will be impressed by the fact that their parents will back them even if they are stepping into the adulthood stage, thus inspiring them to act more actively.

Activity 3. Complete and address the speech.

Were you a representative student, please address the speech after completing it individually.

Good afternoon, dear teachers and parents. Hearing what our headmaster and the parent said, I feel the coming-of-age ceremony exceedingly meaningful.

For me, like my peer fellows, I finally figure out the reason _____ we need this ceremony, which is a kind of formal occasion which shows us we are becoming grown-ups. For our coming-of-age, there is no need for us to draw back because our parents will be on the scene _____ they will offer us countless support. Please believe us, dear parents and teachers. We will spare no efforts to become qualified citizens.

All my fellows, please remember today, May 4th, 2021, _____ we are walking on the stage to become adults.

【Design intention】By completing the speech, students will be provided the related context to internalize the attributive clauses introduced by when, where and why. Meanwhile, students are offered a chance to learn how to use the structure effectively in an open atmosphere. It also lays a foundation of the last news report.

Activity 4. Do an interview in pair work.

Were you the reporter from the School News Center, you would interview the student delivering the speech.

The reporter: Thanks for your speech, so why we need to remember May 4th, 2021?

The student: ...

The reporter: Do we need to draw back? Why?

The student：...

The reporter：Can't agree with you more.Thank you.

The student：My pleasure.

Attention：

The students who act as the interviewed ones should use the attributive clauses introduced by when, where and why. The answers are based on the speech.

【Design intention】By filling in the blanks in pairs, students will be provided the related context to check if they really know the structures of the attributive clauses introduced by when, where and why. And then internalize the grammar themselves. By performing the interview, students are offered another chance to consolidate what they've learned. At the same time they are inspired to think about their own inner thoughts.

Activity 5. Writing.

Were you the reporter from the School News Center, please report the content of the speeches and the interview using the attributive clauses learnde by when, where, why to make other students know the coming-of-age.

Group discussion：

1. What are the main content of the interview and the two speeches?

2. How do you feel about the coming-of-age?

Attention：

1. Please try to use the attributive clauses introduced by when, where, and why as many as possible.

2. Every correct attributive clause is worth 20 points.

【Design intention】This part is designed to help students to put what they have learned into practical use. Meanwhile, students are expected to express themselves in English correctly by using the target grammar, which is indispensable for them to form an English thinking mode and understand the difference between Chinese and English better.

Step 3. Presentation.

Two students are invited to share their report and others try to make a correction and give scores they deserve.

Step 4. Homework.

1. Polish your report according to the comments given by your classmates and teacher.

2. Exchange your report with your classmates to improve each other.

Step 5. Conclusion—the closing remarks.

The coming age is the stage <u>when</u> we become somebody who we want to be.

【Design intention】The sentence including what have been reviewed in this class is used to inspire students to become those who they want to be.

第三节　介词+which / whom引导的定语从句

教学设计——自然灾难

Step 1. Watch a short video.

【Design intention】The short video is about the terrible flood in Zhengzhou to arouse the interest of the students and also introduce the topic of this class.

Step 2. Listen and fill.

Everybody！Watch out for the extreme rainfall and the rainfall is storming into the subway. In other words，the reason for _____ we watch out for the rainfall is that it is tremendously flooding into the subway. The amount of the rain swells to the warning level and it causes the flood-stricken area，for _____ Henan becomes a world focus. Namely，the rain swells to the warning level，as a result of _____，Henan becomes a world focus because of the flood-stricken area. Luckily，the soldiers are sent here. They spare no efforts to save the trapped ones in the tube. That is to say，they spare no efforts to save the trapped ones in the tube，to _____ we are grateful. Finally，after the soldiers selflessly worked for hours，their effort paid off. Many passengers have been rescued. To be brief, the soldiers selflessly worked for hours, for _____ we extremely appreciate.

【Design intention】The purpose of listening to the clip is to introduce the teaching target, the attributive clauses introduced by prep+which/whom in this class. Students are expected to fill in the blanks with related relatives which and whom by listening practice.

Step 3. Ask and answer.

1. What is the reason for which we should watch out?

2. What is the result of the rain swelling to the warning level?

3. For what we extremely appreciate?

【Design intention】By observing and answering the questions, students will have a basic understanding of the attributive clauses introduced by prep+which/whom. During this period, students are encouraged to find out the answers using attributive clauses introduced by prep+which/whom as well.

Step 4. Complete the interviews and do a role-play.

Work in groups to fill in the blanks to complete the two interviews.

Interview 1: the rescue workers and the reporter

The reporter: Thanks for your efforts. Can you describe the subway's situation for us?

The rescue worker A: It's my duty to do so. Actually, the subway by _____ thousands of passengers went home was filled with water.

The reporter: Many thanks to you. Would you please introduce the passengers' situation to us?

The rescue worker B: When arriving there, we found that the light from many cellphones, through _____ passengers were comforting each other played an important role.

Interview 2: the passengers and the reporter

The reporter: God bless you. What's your feeling when you were faced with the rainfall?

The passenger A: Nothing could be better than being rescued by the rescue workers, _____ whom I am grateful.

The reporter: What do you want to say now?

The passenger B: The experience reminds me that life is precious. I need to live well in every second. More importantly, the soldiers tried their best to save us, for I exceedingly appreciate.

The reporter: At present, about 25 were dead as rains deluged in China's flood-stricken central province of Henan. The rescue team were sent there to save those trapped continuously, about _____ we will pay close attention. Hope those encountering the flood can come to life as soon as possible.

【Design intention】 Filling in the blanks, students will be provided the related context to learn the usages of prep+ which/whom in attributive clauses effectively. At the same time they are inspired to cherish the opportunity to live well and appreciate the efforts made by the rescue workers and the soldiers, thus arousing their emotion to express their gratitude.

Step 5. Read and fill.

I've never thought that I would encounter the experience, as a consequence of _____, I will cherish every second in my rest of life. The heavy rainfall tremendously struck Zhengzhou, because of _____ Henan was record-breaking in China. Fortunately, soldiers came to rescue us, with the efforts of _____, we were finally sent to safe areas. Undoubtedly, the soldiers' devotion was worth a praise, to _____ we are extremely grateful.

Needless to say, I exceptionally treasure the chance to survive from the flood, as a result of _____, I understand that living well matters most. Consequently, treasure all you've possessed.

【Design intention】 The purpose of filling in the blanks individually is to help students consolidate what they have learned in this class. Meanwhile, reading this blog enables students to arouse their inner emotion for appreciating life, namely "using English to express what we want to convey to others".

Step 6. Writing.

If you were a reporter from CCTV-9, you would report the news to us. Please compose a report which includes：

1. the flood situation in the subway

2. the feelings of the interviewees

3. a conclusion from the blog

Attention：

1. Please try to use the attributive clauses introduced by prep+which/whom as many as possible.

2. Every correct attributive clause is worth 20 points.

【Design intention】This part is designed to help students to put what they have learned into practical use. Meanwhile，students are expected to express themselves in English correctly by using the target grammar，which is indispensable for them to form an English thinking mode and understand the difference between Chinese and English better.

Step 7. Presentation.

Two students are invited to share their reports covering the flood situation in the subway，the feelings of the interviewees and a conclusion from the blog in front of the class.

Step 8. Homework.

1. Polish your report and exchange it with your deskmate.

2. Conclusion—the closing remark.

We never know what is gonna happen tomorrow，as a consequence of which，live life to the fullest right here right now.

【Design intention】The sentence including what have been learnt in this class is used to inspire students，which calls on students to cherish life，thus making them realize they are supposed to live life to the fullest.

第四节 定语从句复习

教学设计——全运会

Step 1. Lead in：The activity before the class.

Let's recall something proud together. Do you remember what was the biggest event that happened in Xi'an in September 2021?

Q1：What are the word the "biggest" and the sentence structure "that happened" used to do?

Q2：Do you know other relative words besides "that" in attributive clauses?

【Design intention】Use the 14th National Games as the lead-in to arouse students' interest, leading students to get involved in the teaching target as they answer the two questions above—the revision of attributive clauses in this class. Simultaneously, students will be led to review the relative words they remember.

Step 2. The activities during the class.

Activity 1. Fill and report.

If you were the reporter from Shaanxi TV, you would address the opening report.

This is Shaanxi TV live show. Welcome to the 14th National Games closing ceremony, _____ is being held in Xi'an now. As you can see, audience on the spot are very excited. This is a nationwide event _____ we are looking forward to. Given a chance to interview the players, I, as the reporter, will choose those _____ I admire most. What about you?

【Design intention】Based on the opening report of the closing ceremony, the attributive clauses will be shown to students, during which, students will be familiar with the basic relative words such as who, whom, that and which. Meanwhile, students are looking forward to what will happen next.

Activity 2. Fill and interview.

Were you the reporter and the local audience，please do the interview in pairs.

The Reporter：Welcome to be on the spot. Where are you from?

The Audience：I come from Xi'an _____ the 14th National Games was held.

The Reporter：So do you know the reason _____ it was held in Xi'an?

The Audience：I guess the reason is that Xi'an is qualified for it both economically and culturally.

The Reporter：What about the time _____ the volleyball competition was held?

The Audience：Six days ago. It's awesome.

The Reporter：Definitely.

【Design intention】By filling in the blanks，students will get familiar with relative words such as when，where and why. Involved in the activity，students will be proud of the fact that the 14th National Games was held in Xi'an，thus inspiring them to act more actively.

Activity 3. Complete and address the speech.

Were you Zhuting，please address the speech after completing it individually.

I feel extremely honored to deliver the speech，in _____ I'd like to express my thanks and determination. As you can see，Shaanxi has made every effort to make the event held successfully，for _____ we athletes are grateful tremendously. Needless to say，people here take the responsibility to make everything smooth and well-organized，to _____ I'm grateful. From the bottom of my heart，I，representing all the athletes，make up our minds to try our best，keeping the athletic spirit going on.

【Design intention】By completing the speech，students will be provided the related context to review the structure "prep+which/whom" in the attributive clauses. Meanwhile，students are offered a chance to learn how to use the structure effectively in an open atmosphere. At the same time，students are aware of the contributions Shaanxi did for the 14th National Games, which also offers a stage for students to be proud of their city through learning English and lays a foundation of the last conclusion report.

Activity 4. Deliver an official speech.

Were you the officer from the 14th National Games Committee, please deliver the speech after filling in the blanks in groups.

Good evening, ladies and gentlemen, athletes and judges. Welcome to the ancient city, Xi'an. _____ is known to us, Xi'an is a city with a long history. I do believe you have been impressed by people and culture here. _____ is widely recognized, the 14th National Games _____ aim is to show the athletic development of our nation has inherited the spirit of cooperative teamwork and athletic power. _____ you can see, Shaanxi develops so prosperously, economy and culture keep up with the pace of other provinces like Henan and Jiangxi. It proves that the Communist Party of China _____ policies focus on people's life leads us to a brighter future.

【Design intention】By completing the speech cooperatively, students will be provided the related context to review the relative words "as" and "whose". Meanwhile, students will be provided opportunities to learn how to use the structure effectively in an open atmosphere. At the same time they are encouraged to take an active part in the activities. Simultaneously, students are cultivated to be grateful to our great motherland. Without the correct guidance of the Communist Party of China, such great changes and development wouldn't take place, thus arousing them to show their love and passion for our own country. Also, it is indispensable to students for their final language outcome.

Activity 5. Writing

Were you the reporter, please write a conclusion report using attributive clauses.

Be sure to include the following points:

1. The main content of the interview and the two speeches.

2. Your feelings about the closing ceremony.

Group discussion：

1. What are the main content of the interview and the two speeches?

2. How do you feel about the closing ceremony ?

Attention：

1. Please try to use attributive clauses as many as possible.

2. Every correct attributive clause is worth 20 points.

【Design intention】This part is designed to help students to put what they have learned into practical use. Meanwhile，students are expected to express themselves in English correctly by using the target grammar，which is indispensable for them to form an English thinking mode and understand the difference between Chinese and English better.

Step 3. Presentation.

Two students are invited to share their conclusion reports and others try to make a correction and give scores they deserve.

Step 4. Homework.

1. Polish your conclusion report to make it a better one.

2. Share your report with your classmates.

Step 5. Conclusion—the closing remarks.

1. God helps those who help themselves.

2. We are so lucky to live in the peaceful years when we can pursue our dreams heart and soul.

【Design intention】The two sentences including what have been reviewed in this class are used to inspire students. For the first one，it calls on students to work hard. For the second one，it cultivates students to be grateful to our great motherland for what the Communist Party of China has done for us，thus making them realize they are supposed to achieve their dreams heart and soul.

第二章

名词性从句教学设计

第一节　名词性从句作宾语和表语

教学设计一——英语学习

Step 1. Lead-in.

Teacher：Do you like English? I want to talk about English learning with you in this class.

Step 2. Presentation.

The teacher asks one student to retell what he/she asked and show the sentences：

The teacher asked whether we liked English.

The teacher asked why we liked English.

The teacher said that he/she wanted to...

Students complete the chart by observing and analyzing the sentences above.

object clause	relatives	sentence element and meaning
declarative sentence	+ that	not used as any element；no meaning
general question	+ _____	not used as any element；the event is certain/uncertain
special question	who，whom，what	subject
	which，whose	
	when，where，how，why	

【Design intention】By observing and analyzing the sentences，students will have a basic understanding of the function and usage of object clauses，especially the function of the conjunctions.

Step 3. Practice.

Teacher：The other day，one of my students，Li Hua had a talk with me about English learning.

1. Complete the dialogue with the conjunctions.

Li Hua：Hello，Vanya. I have been so sad recently. Shall we have a talk?

Vanya：Sure.

Li Hua：I have been thinking about _____ I could improve my English, but I don't know _____ I should do.

Vanya：First of all，I want to know _____ you are interested in English.

Li Hua：Em...I can tell you honestly _____ I am not very interested because it is not easy for me. I always wonder _____ the other students can do so well in English. Is it because they are talented? I even doubt _____ I should give it up.

Vanya：Don't be so negative. Remember _____ I said? Never give up! Have you turned to your classmates for advice?

Li Hua：Yes. I once asked Xiaoming to help me decide _____ dictionary suits me best.

Vanya：Good. Don't worry about it too much. I believe _____ once you make every effort，you will make progress.

2. Students work in pairs to make the dialogue and check the answers with each other.

3. The teacher invites a student to present the dialogue as well as check the answers with the whole class.

【Design intention】This is a controlled exercise in which students are required to complete the dialogue with conjunctions, and by doing so they will be aware of the function of the conjunctions and use them correctly.

Step 4. Writing.

Supposing you are Li Hua，you have some difficulty in English learning. Please write a letter to your teacher about it and try to use as many object clauses as possible.

1. Useful sentence patterns

I wonder/doubt/...

I have been think about...

I don't know...

I hope/believe...

Can you tell me...

2. Linking words：besides，what's more，moreover，in addition...

Dear Vanya，

Knowing that you are willing to help me with my English，I am writing this letter for help.

First of all，I wonder _____

_____

_____

_____

_____

_____

_____

Thank you for your patience. I do hope you can give me some advice.

Yours，

Li Hua

After writing，some students will be invited to share their letters about some difficulties in English learning.

【Design intention】Through this less-controlled activity, students will be able to integrate what they've learned in previous activities to write a letter for help, so that they will have their comprehensive competences developed.

Step 5. Self-assessment.

In this lesson,

1. I have learned the form and usage of object clauses.   Yes./No.

2. I can use the conjunctions properly (that, whether/if, who, whom, what, which, whose, where, how, why).   Yes./No.

3. I am able to write a letter asking for help by using object clauses.   Yes./No.

4. I think I could do better if I made every effort.   Yes./No.

【Design intention】In this part, students will reflect on what they've learned in this class and know how to make improvements in future learning.

Step 6. Homework.

1. Polish your letter.

2. Exchange it with your classmates to talk about more ways on how to learn English well.

教学设计二——学生郊游

Step 1. Lead-in.

The teacher shows some pictures about the hiking held last Monday and gives his/her introduction to the preparation for the activity and some ideas about it.

We just finished a 22-kilometer-hiking from our school to the Ankang Fuqiang Airport. In fact, it took the school leaders two weeks to discuss where we would go, when we would go, how we would go and what we should do for the hiking. When we were told (that) we would go to the airport on foot and plant some trees on March 22nd, we were worried about whether you were able to cover such a long distance. But to my surprise, when Mr. Yang asked who would ask a day off and not participate in the activity in our class, nobody gave up and all of you were determined to challenge yourselves. We were happy that everyone in our class could overcome all the difficulties and that all of you behaved very well in the activity. Actually, I think (that) no season is more pleasant than spring and that it was such a fine day to go hiking. Of course, I found (that) all of us enjoyed ourselves a lot.

【Design intention】The purpose of the passage is to arouse the students' interest and to introduce the teaching target, the noun clauses as the object in this class.

Step 2. Pair work.

Ask the students to work in pairs to underline all the clauses and remind them to pay attention to the colored words, then ask them to answer the following questions according to the passage.

1. What did the leaders discuss before the hiking?

They discussed _____.

2. What were our teachers worried bout?

They were worried about _____.

3. What made our teacher surprised?

He/She was surprised _____.

4. Why were they happy?

They were happy (to see) _____.

5. How does our teacher think of spring?

He/She thinks _____.

【Design intention】The purpose of pair work is to lead the students to use object clauses. This activity is also aimed to train the students' ability of analyzing and summarizing information. Their awareness of cooperation is developed as well.

Step 3. Free talk.

According to the given questions as follows, ask the students to use object clauses as possible as they can.

1. What were you worried about before the hiking?

I was worried about...

For example: I was worried about whether we could cover such a long walk.

I was worried about whether we would get sunburnt or not.

2. What did you see or hear during the hiking?

I saw/heard...

For example: I saw that the fields were full of golden rape flowers and lovely green wheat.

I heard some students reciting poems along the road and that our teachers kept encouraging us to go on.

3. What have you learned from the activity?

I learned...

For example: I learned that hiking is a good way to get close to nature and exercise ourselves as well.

I learned that it is of great importance to persist and cooperate with each other in a challenging task.

【Design intention】The purpose of the free talk is to open students' mind to talk about the activity, which can serve as a preparation for the later writing. It also gives students a chance to use object clauses again in oral expressions.

Step 4. Writing.

Based on what have been talked just now, ask the students to work in groups of four to write a diary. Try to use object clauses as possible as they can.

【Design intention】The purpose of the writing is to help students express themselves clearly and logically as well as use object clauses in written English. Writing belongs to the output of language learning and is aimed to test how much students have mastered what they have learned in this period.

Step 5. Presentation.

Choose two or four groups to present their diaries to the whole class, and guide students to do peer evaluation based on the following points:

1. Does the diary cover object clauses?   Yes./No.

2. Were the relatives used properly (that, whether/if, who, whom, what, which, whose, where, how, why)?   Yes./No.

3. Was the diary well-organized by using object clauses?   Yes./No.

【Design intention】The purpose of the presentation is to give students chances to show themselves, which can build up their confidence. At the same time, they also have chances to learn from others, which can give them much help to improve their own writing later.

Step 6. Homework.

Polish your diary and hand it in.

The sample by the teacher：

Last Monday, all the teachers and students in our school had a 22-kilometer-hiking from our school to the Ankang Fuqiang Airport.

We gathered on the playground at 7：30 in the morning. After an-hour opening ceremony, we set off in lines with the lead of our teachers. Excited and relaxed, we were walking as we were singing and admiring the beautiful scenery along the road. We saw the leaves turn green and that the fields were full of golden rape flowers and lovely green wheat. We saw the colorful butterflies and busy bees were dancing over the flowers. On arriving at the airport, we had a close look at the modern and well-furnished airport. We cooperated to plant many trees beside the airport. We were glad to see each of them was named a significant name by us. Later, we enjoyed lunch provided by the staff in our school canteen. Hungry and tired, although the lunch was simple, we found we had never had such a more delicious lunch before. Around 6 o'clock in the afternoon, we came back on foot, exhausted but fulfilled.

We all think highly of this hiking and consider it a good way to get close to nature and exercise ourselves as well. If time permits, I am looking forward to having more chances to take part in more such activities.

教学设计三——名著赏析

Step 1. Lead-in：Guess an ancient Chinese story from the following dialogue.

"I know which of you is the real Sun Wukong. But I won't say who he is. I won't tell the truth because the question is that the fake Sun Wukong has all the same power as the real one. If I point him out，he will be angry and destroy the entire palace. That is why I cannot speak the truth in public." said Curious Ear（谛听）.

——*Two Wukongs* from *Journey to the West*

【Design intention】A guessing game is used to introduce the students to a certain situation and arouse students' interest as well.

Step 2. Read and analyze：Read the following sentences from the passage and try to figure out their structures and constituents.

1. I know which of you is the real Sun Wukong.

2. But I won't say who he is.

3. The question is that the fake Sun Wukong has all the same power as the real one.

4. That is why I cannot speak the truth in public.

5. Guan Yin thinks that only the real Wukong will get a headache when she recites the spell（念咒语）.

6. Lord Lao Zi（太上老君）has some doubt whether the fake Wukong will be burnt to ashes in his Eight Trigrams Furnace（八卦炉）.

7. Curious Ear suggests（that）the two Wukongs fly to where the Buhhda（佛祖）lives to seek the truth.

8. The time when the fake Wukong disappears is when the Bohhda sees through everything in his inner world.

9. The Jade Emperor（玉帝）gets furious because he neither knows how he could distinguish the two Wukongs nor stops them damaging the Sky Court.

Discovery：

1. I know which of you is the real Sun Wukong.（noun clause used as object）

2. But I won't say who he is.（noun clause used as object）

3. The question is that the fake Sun Wukong has all the same power as the real one.（noun clause used as predicative）

4. That is why I cannot speak the truth in public.（noun clause used as predicative）

5. Guan Yin thinks that only the real Wukong will get a headache when she recites the spell.（noun clause used as object）

6. Lord Lao Zi（太上老君）doubts whether the fake Wukong will be burnt to ashes in his Eight Trigrams Furnace（八卦炉）.（noun clause used as object）

7. Curious Ear suggests（that）the two Wukongs fly to where the Buhhda lives to seek the truth.（noun clause used as object）

8. The time when the fake Wukong disappears is when the Bohhda sees through everything in his inner world.（noun clause used as predicative）

9. The Jade Emperor gets furious because he neither knows how he could distinguish the two Wukongs nor stops them damaging the Sky Court.（noun clause used as object）

【Design intention】In this part，students will have a basic understanding of what noun clauses are used as objects and predicatives through observation and discovery, and then they will have the ability to conclude some basic rules and try to use them if necessary.

Step 3. Practice.

Activity 1. Fill in the blanks with proper conjunctives and recognize whether the sentences are object or predicative clauses.

1. Guan Yin can't tell <u>which</u> of the two Wukongs is real because they all feel pain when she recites the spell.（object clause）

2. The Jade Emperor is angry for the two Wukongs because the fact is <u>that</u> they are fighting and damaging his Sky Court.（predicative clause）

3. The question for Curious Ear is <u>whether</u> it can tell the truth to the public.（predicative clause）

4. The Jade Emperor is tired of <u>what</u> Wukongs have done for his Sky Court.（object clause）

5. Wujing knows <u>where</u> Guanyin lives and flies towards her for help.（object clause）

6. The problems remains <u>how</u> they can pick out the fake one from the two Wukongs for everyone.（predicative clause）

7. Curious Ear only tells his owner <u>who</u> is the fake Wukong secretly.（object clause）

8. In front of the Buddha，the real Wukong bows（鞠躬）while the fake one

hesitates <u>whether</u> he should do the same because of his fearness.（<u>object clause</u>）

9. "I know <u>why</u> you are here, and I know <u>which</u> of you is a fake." says Buddha to the fake Wukong.（<u>object clause</u>）

10. The fake Wukong exists <u>when</u> Sun Wukong is disloyal to Tong Monk（唐僧）and his duty.（<u>predicative clause</u>）

Attention：

Every group leader speaks out their introduction and each correct answer would gain 1 point.

Activity 2. Read the whole sentences in class and other students decide whether they are correct sentences.

Activity 3. Debating.

Topic：Couldn't the gods including Lord Lao Zi，the Jade Emperor and Guan Yin indeed tell who is the fake Wukong？And why do they choose to be silent to the public？（Each correct noun clause spoken will add 1 point to your team.）

For example：

Pros：I think that all the gods know who is the fake one clearly and the reason why they don't let the secret out is that they are afraid of offending someone else.

Cons：I don't think all the gods have the idea of who is the real Wukong because the fake one can do what the real one does in every respect...

【Design intention】After summarizing the theoretical rules of object and predicative clauses，it is high time that the students should get a lot of practice to consolidate their practical ability. Additionally，in this positively competitive atmosphere，students are more likely to learn the features and structures of noun clauses effectively.

Step 4. Rewriting and presentation.

Rewrite the chapter *Two Wukongs* with as many noun clauses as possible.

One day，Wujing sees two Wukongs both claim they are the real but he can't realize _____ . He thinks Guanyin may be able to distinguish _____ . So he flies to where _____ and tells what _____ . Unfortunately，Guanyin doesn't know _____ because the fact is _____ . Then they turn to the Jade Emperor for help. He tells the two monkeys _____ because the most furious thing for him is _____. They have to go to the Land of Dark（地府）and believe Curious Ear knows _____. Unexpectedly, the god beast says _____. Finally, they turn to the Buddha and hope _____. Being afraid of the Buddha's power, the fake Wukong _____ ...

【Design intention】In this part, students have the opportunities to use and present their understanding of the grammar they have learned in the whole class when they will enhance their comprehension ability of noun clauses and build their confidence in learning grammar. Hopefully, this part will help them arouse their cultural sense in "using English to tell stories of our Chinese" and their creative thinking will be developed in the meanwhile.

Step 5. Conclusion.

Let students try to conclude what they have learned in this class in their own words, and additional and correctional comments are highly welcomed.

【Design intention】In another perspective, students will survey what they have learned in the class rationally and be improved by giving and accepting comments, thus having a better understanding of this class.

Step 6. Homework.

1. Review the grammar points learned in this class.

2. Polish your rewriting with partners, paying attention to using the correct conjunctions.

【Design intention】Homework is used to consolidate what students have learned and also help different levels of the students to get something useful in this class.

教学设计四——毕业典礼

Step 1. Lead-in：Listen and fill in the blanks.

Honorable teachers, dear parents and students,

Good morning to you all. On this sunny and unforgettable day, we overwhelmingly welcome you all to our graduation ceremony.

Three years ago, you were immature teenagers, but now you are not _____ you used to be.You have understood _____ counts most during your youth. Actually, what your parents pay close attention to is not only _____ you have gained knowledge or not but also care about _____ much you can get from your study experiences. As headmaster, I, as well as my colleagues constantly remind ourselves _____ responsibility is indeed a virtue and a necessity. Consequently, we are always inspired by _____ is rooted in our mind regardless of understanding or misunderstanding. Thankfully, you have achieved _____ you have sought for. I'm pretty sure _____ nothing would happen if we teachers hadn't put our heart into your study and growth.

In conclusion, I am convinced _____ you will apply the utmost knowledge to the development of society under the guidance of your reliable peers, your honorable teachers and your dear parents. Congratulations on your graduation.

【Design intention】The purpose of listening to the clip is to introduce the teaching target— the noun clauses as the object and predictive in this class. Students are expected to fill in the blanks with related conjunctions such as what, that, how and whether introducing the object clauses and predictive clauses by listening practice.

Step 2. Pair work: Work in pairs to ask and answer the following questions.

1. What have the students understood?

The students have understood that _____.

2. Do the parents just pay close attention to knowledge? why?

_____.

3. What are the teachers and headmaster inspired by?

_____.

4. What is headmaster pretty sure?

_____.

【Design intention】By observing and answering the questions, students will have a basic understanding of the object clauses and predictive clauses. During this period，students are encouraged to be familiar with the sentence structure as well.

Step 3. Read the speech，fill in blanks and do an interview.

Activity 1. Work in groups：Fill in the blanks to complete the speech.

Respectable headmaster，dear parents and students，

Good morning to you all. I am honored to deliver a graduation speech today. At the time of being admitted as a member of qualified teachers，I，as well as all my colleagues solemnly（庄严地）promise/swear to pursue _____ we have been longing for，which means _____ we will always spare no efforts to be someone who is talented，elegant，capable，helpful，earnest and reliable.

Actually，dear students，you really motivate us teachers to never doubt _____ it's worthwhile to take up this job or not because we feel _____ it is an urge to do so. Even we have encountered rough patches during the teaching process，we still love _____ we are doing. Dear parents，you undoubtedly pave the way for _____ _____ your kids need for their study. You know _____ it is the proper time to offer a cup of tea or a bar of chocolate. Dear colleagues，we all proceed this profession with conscience and responsibility，so we will be remembered and appreciated for _____ we have done.

Today，my dear students，you will turn over a new chapter of your lives and you will walk towards the light of the glory tomorrow.

Activity 2. Pair work：Recite the speech again and do the interview.

（Student A and Student B take turns to act as the Teacher and the Host.）

Attention：

The students who answer the questions should use the object clauses or predictive clauses.

An interview：

Host：Thank you for your speech. Can I ask you three questions?

Teacher：Absolutely.

Host：What do you teachers pursue?

Teacher：...

Host：What is your pursuit?

Teacher：...

Host：Have you ever doubt whether it's worthwhile to be a teacher?

Teacher：...

Host：Thank you again. Good day to you.

【Design intention】For the activity 1, by filling in the blanks, students will be provided the related context to cooperatively learn the structure of object clauses and predictive clauses effectively. For the activity 2, by answering the questions, students are offered a chance to consolidate what they've internalized and digested. Hence, students will be provided opportunities to learn how to use the object clauses and predictive clauses effectively in an open atmosphere. At the same time they are encouraged to take an active part in the activities and aroused to show gratitude to their teachers.

Step 4. Practice：Read another speech, fill in the blanks and do an interview.

Activity 1. Work individually：Fill in the blanks to complete the speech.

Honorable headmaster, teachers and dear kids,

I'm honored to be with you today at your graduation ceremony. I have every reason to believe _____ you, dear teachers, are the most respectable figures and _____ you, dear kids, are the most fortunate students.

From the bottom of my heart, I deeply appreciate _____ all the teachers have offered for the kids. I'm extremely sure _____ none of this would happen if you hadn't devoted your full energy to educating these kids. You have fulfilled _____ you have pursued even though you don't know _____ kind of students they are or _____ their characteristics are. Words fail to convey _____ I want to express. If allowed, I'd like to invite all the kids to say "thank you, honorable teachers." Dear kids, as a Chinese poem reads, "When one is in his office, he should discharge his duty conscientiously". Therefore, _____ you are supposed to do is _____ you need to make the best of your college life. Wish all of you possess a bright future.

Activity 2. Pair work：Recite the speech again and do the interview.

（Student A and Student B take turns to act as the Parent and the Host.）

Host：Thank you for your speech. May I ask you several questions?

Parent：Sure.

Host：What do you deeply appreciate for the teachers?

Parent：...

Host：What are you extremely sure?

Parent：...

Host：What do you think the students are supposed to do?

Parent：...

Host：Thank you again.

Attention：

The students who answer the questions should use the object clauses or predictive clauses.

【Design intention】For the activity 1, by filling in the blanks individually, again students will be provided the related context to get familiar with the structures of object clauses and predictive clauses by thinking independently and then internalize the two kinds of clauses themselves. For the activity 2, by performing the interview, students are offered a chance to consolidate what they've internalized. At the same time they are inspired to think about their own inner thoughts, thus arousing their emotion to express gratitude to their parents.

Step 5. Writing.

If you are given a chance to deliver a speech at the graduation ceremony, please compose a graduation speech.

Attention：

1. Please try to use object clauses and predictive clauses as many as possible.

2. Every correct object clause or predictive clause is worth 10 points.

【Design intention】This part is designed to help students to put what they have learned into practical use. Meanwhile, students are expected to express themselves in English correctly by using the grammar, which is indispensable for them to form an English thinking mode and understand the difference between Chinese and English better.

Step 6. Presentation.

Two students are invited to share their speech in the class.

Step 7. Homework.

1. Polish your speech if there is any mistake.

2. Read your speech to your classmates.

第二节　名词性从句作主语

教学设计一——月球之旅

Step 1. Lead-in：Watch and enjoy.

Last month，I had a visit to the moon with my friend，now it's time to share the video of the visit with you.

【Design intention】The topic of the video is about a visit to the moon，which is also the topic of the previous reading in this unit，so it is designed to be the background of this grammar learning to pave the way for students' understanding. Besides，it aims to stimulate students' enthusiasm in this class.

Step 2. Listen and answer.

Let's have a look at what happened exactly.

1. What surprised me as we left the earth?

2. The weight lessened，but I was nervous extremely. Why?

3. What was my feeling when I was in space?

4. What surprised me when I was on the moon?

5. Who will love the trip to the moon? Man or woman? Child or adult?

6. What is being discussed?

【Design intention】The purpose of listening to the clip is to introduce the teaching target—noun clauses as the subject in this class. Students are encouraged to find out the answers expressed with the subject clauses to the questions about the visit to the moon by listening practice.

Step 3. Read and check

Last month, I visited the moon with my friend. As we left the earth, I became very heavy. How the force of gravity changed surprised me. Gradually, the weight lessened. However, when the force of gravity would disappear was unknown, so I was nervous extremely. Luckily, when I was in space, what made me nervous disappeared. We floated weightlessly and I cheered up. When I was on the moon, that walking needs lots of practice surprised me. Returning to the earth was very frightening, and we were exhausted but very excited. Whoever goes to the moon will love the trip. To my delight, which star will be the next destination is being discussed. (听力材料)

【Design intention】In this part, students are expected to read the listening material to check their answers in step 2, actually, which is the reappearance and reinforcement of the knowledge point and aims to help students understand the subject clauses again by reading.

Step 4. Read and enjoy.

Activity 1. Read the answers (subject clauses) and focus.

1. How the force of gravity changed surprised me.

2. When the force of gravity would disappear was unknown.

3. What made me nervous disappeared.

4. That walking needs lots of practice surprised me.

5. Whoever goes to the moon will love the trip.

6. Which star will be the next destination is being discussed.

Activity 2. Enjoy (the splendid moment we experienced on the moon) and complete.

When we got closer to the moon gradually was exciting. _____ the earth became smaller and the moon larger cheered me. _____ scene was most shocking was unknown for my friend. However, _____ amazed me most was the outburst of the fire on the outside of the spaceship. _____ we got the hang of walking on the moon was not important, we enjoyed ourselves. _____ knew about our trip to the moon was surprised.

【Design intention】In the activity 1, students are supposed to read the answers expressed with subject clauses and focus on the conjunctions to understand and feel the rules of subject clauses. And then, students are expected to complete the sentences in the activity 2 after their understanding. The activities can help them to understand the basic structure of the noun clauses as the subject introduced by that, whether, who, whom, which, what, whose, where, when, why and how step by step.

Step 5. Practice.

Life is different on a spaceship. There is very little gravity, so things float around. Make a discussion about your visit to the moon.

Activity 1. Make subject clauses in pairs according to the information given below.

Problems	Things
① how to breathe	① oxygen tanks
② what to dress	② spacesuit
③ what to eat	③ space food
④ how to travel	④ space buggy

Requirements：

1. Each pair needs to make at least one sentence.

2. Every student must use subject clauses to talk.

Example：

1. How we breathe on the moon is the most important consideration.

2. That oxygen tanks must be taken is necessary.

3. What we should dress is the spacesuit.

4. What we can eat on the moon should be discussed.

Activity 2. Have a discussion in groups about the visit to the moon.

Requirements：

1. Each group needs to make at least one dialogue.

2. At least two subject clauses must be contained in your dialogue.

Example：

S1：I am excited that we can have a travel to the moon, but we may encounter some problems. What do you think?

S2：Yes. In my opinion, how we breathe on the moon is the most important consideration.

S3：That oxygen tanks must be taken is necessary. Besides oxygen tanks, what we should dress is also a problem. What is your opinion, S4?

S4：From my perspective, what we should dress is the spacesuit.

【Design intention】By making subject clauses and the dialogue, students can get a better understanding step by step, which is helpful to build their confidence. Meanwhile, the different levels of difficulty in two activities correspond to different levels of students, which can make students more interested and active to be involved in the class.

Step **6**. Writing.

Supposing your friend Remi will have a visit to the moon, she hopes you can give her some suggestions. Please try to write a short passage according to the discussion above.

Attention：

1. Please try to use subject clauses as many as possible.

2. Every correct subject clause is worth 10 points.

【Design intention】This part is designed to help students to use what they have learned in an organized way. Meanwhile, students are expected to convert Chinese to English correctly by using the grammar, which is helpful for them to form an English thinking mode and understand the difference between Chinese and English better.

Step **7**. Presentation.

Two students are invited to share their suggestions about the visit to the moon.

Step **8**. Homework.

Polish your suggestions according to the comments given by your classmates and teacher and hand it in.

教学设计二——脱贫攻坚

Step 1. Lead-in：The new year speech.

The year 2021 is arriving. The president Xi Jinping sent the new year speech to the whole nation. Let's watch the video and listen to what he said.

1. In 2020，what we got is a historic accomplishment in fighting against rural poverty.

2. That the efforts of the folks and the contribution of the poverty-eradication workers（扶贫工作者）made often comes to my mind.

3. How we steadily march ahead towards common prosperity is still our goal.

4. Whether we can make further progress and when more "Stories of Spring" will be created depend on our joint efforts.

5. What astonished the whole world is that through 8 years，China has made 100 million rural people affected out of poverty and 832 poor countries have got rid of poverty.

【Design intention】In this lead-in，some good sentences are from the president's new year speech，which are designed to be the background of this grammar learning to pave the way for students' understanding. Besides，it aims to stimulate students' enthusiasm in this class. Students will get the basic understanding about subject clauses by listening to Xi's speech.

Step 2. Out of poverty—the warmest Chinese story.

The president Xi said that the efforts of the folks and the contributions of the poverty-eradication workers（扶贫工作者）often came to his mind. Let's listen to their stories.

Fan Jianwu：Three big decisions.

When he was 17 years old，dropping out of school was his first decision. Why he made such a decision puzzled everyone. But what he wanted was to start his own business to get the burden off his family. In 2009，what he decided was to return to his village and become a director of his village. At that time, that his own company was making progress made him hesitated. Finally, he made the third decision, selling his company and raising funds. Whether his hard work would pay off was unknown. What he could do was to persuade house by house to plant trees. Nowadays, the whole villagers succeed in getting rid of poverty.

Su Li: If poverty is a disease, love is the best solution.

In 2003, she was assigned to work in a village. Meanwhile, what she faced was her daughter who would be left alone. When the work would come to an end was unknown, maybe a lifetime. That the girl Yuan Yuan was in rags made her sad. How she could help the girl get more care and love filled her heart. The girl asked Su Li:

"Are you willing to be my mother? " Whoever heard the words would be heart-broken. In 2018, Yuan Yuan's family successfully got themselves rid of poverty with Su Li's help.

【Design intention】In Step 1, Xi refers to the fight against poverty, so in Step 2, students will get a chance to know how people struggled to get out of poverty by reading two warm stories about the fight against poverty. The story is the reappearance and reinforcement of the target grammar and aims to help students understand subject clauses again by reading.

Step 3. Fill and share.

After the president Xi gave his new year speech, the fight against poverty has become a hot topic on the Internet. Netizens have given their opinions and comments. After knowing the stories about the fight against poverty, what is your feeling?

Activity 1. Fill in the blanks.

Amy: When the bright future will come is unknown, but I believe it's coming soon.

William: _____ helps the rural people affected out of poverty is our hero.

Gary: There is no shortcut to get rid of poverty, and _____ we should do is to work hard.

Henry: _____ fighting against poverty is not a matter of one person must be known.

Activity 2. Share your opinion in pairs.

My opinion： _____ .

Requirements：

1. Use subject clauses as many as possible.

2. Refer to the information below if you need.

Reference：

1. The firm belief that we should hold.

2. The leadership of the Communist Party of China.

3. The meaning of fighting against poverty.

4. Not a matter of one person.

Example：

What we should do is to unite and work together.

【Design intention】In the activity 1，students are expected to fill in the blanks in the sentences from netizens' comments to understand the rules of subject clauses. And then，students are expected to talk about their opinions in Activity 2. From Activity 1 to Activity 2，it is an exercise from filling in a conjunction to making a new sentence. Meanwhile，it is a chance for students to express what they want to do after knowing the comments about the fight against poverty，which is also a foundation for the next step.

Step 4. Express yourself.

If you have a chance to tell the stories about the fight against poverty around you，what do you want to express to make others know the importance and the meaning of the fight?

Attention：

1. Subject clauses are expected to use.

2. Every correct subject clause is worth 10 points.

3. Each group is expected to have at least three subject clauses.

Example：

My mother told me when she was a little girl，whether she could go to school is a question because of poverty. When they could get enough food to eat was unknown because what she expected at that time was just to fill her stomach. Nowadays, what we need to worry about is not whether we can get enough food to eat but how we can make our life more colorful. In 2020, China got a historic accomplishment in fighting against poverty. In the past several years, the whole nation has been struggling to defeat poverty, which means more and more Chinese will live a better life in the coming years. Why the little girl can not be educated will be no longer a question, and why the folks in rural areas can not step out to see the outside world will be gone forever. What China has got is not only the higher international status but also more respect.

【Design intention】In the previous steps, students have got some information about the fight against poverty and the grammar knowledge, so it's time for students to express themselves by using what they have got. Activities in Step 3 and Step 4 can help students learn more from sentence making to text writing.

Step 5. Presentation.

Two students share their expressions and others try to give some advice to help them make it better.

Step 6. Homework.

Polish your short passage and exchange it with one of your classmates.

教学设计三——读书分享

Step 1. Lead-in: Listen and fill.

_____ is known to us is that reading makes a full man. Hence, _____ we will do in this class is to hold a reading seminar. _____ shares his opinions about his insights from reading is welcomed. _____ you choose eastern or western literature is accepted. _____ you will share is expected to be inspiring, optimistic and appealing. _____ you choose to unfold the mystery of reading completely depends on yourselves.

【Design intention】The purpose of listening to the clip is to introduce the teaching target—noun clauses as the subject in this class. Students are expected to fill in the blanks with related conjunctions such as what, whoever, whether, whatever and how introducing subject clauses by listening practice.

Step 2. Pair work：Ask and answer.

1. What is known to us?

2. What will we do in this class?

3. Can we just choose eastern literature? Why?

【Design intention】By observing and answering the questions, students will have a basic understanding of the subject clauses. During this period, students are encouraged to be familiar with the sentence structure as well.

Step 3. Fill, match and talk.

Activity 1. Fill in the blanks and match the main idea of each book in groups.

Journey to the West	_____ is unfair that God creates someone who is disabled. However, taking an optimistic attitude towards life can light up the sky even in the darkest night. Although she is encountering the physical obstacle by nature, _____ Helen fights against it is to face it fearlessly. _____ we can draw is that we should not be pessimistic about our life no matter what happens.
Three Days to See	It is said _____ a monk is assigned to get the scripture from the Western Heaven with his three students including Sun Wukong, Bajie and Sha Monk. Overcoming numerous blocks, they finally make it. _____ counts most is that the story has inspired us to strive for our dream regardless of fortune or misfortune.
Harry Potter	_____ Harry Potter undergoes seems like a magical journey. _____ is described that Harry has spent 7 years in the Hogwarts School of Witchcraft and Wizardry and become a professional magician. _____ the author expresses is that we are supposed to face the gloomy business bravely.

Activity 2. Free talk（pair work）.

Would you please share more insights about these three masterpieces using one or two subject clauses?

Attention：

Please try your best to use subject clauses.

Following tips may be offered as a reminder.

E.g. 1：It is said/noted/reported/known that+...

E.g. 2：What is known to us is that...

E.g. 3：What matters/counts most is that...

E.g. 4：What attracts/impresses me most is that...

E.g. 5：How she gets through the rough patch is explained in the book.

E.g. 6：Whether Harry Potter becomes a magician or not is revealed finally.

E.g. 7：Whom the magic power belongs to is unknown.

Activity 3. Read a piece of reading insight，fill in the blanks individually and answer questions.

Morning，boys and girls，

It is said _____ some books are to be tasted，others to be swallowed，and some few to be chewed and digested. _____ book you choose may depend on your own preference. _____ histories make men wise, poets witty, the mathematics subtle, natural philosophy deep is known to us.

_____ I'd like to share is my insight from reading a book named *Three Days to See*. Generally，_____ is expected is that readers can be immersed in what the writers intend to express. From this book，_____ is expressed is that we can't choose destiny but we can decide our attitude towards life although it is unfair that God creates someone who is disabled. _____ is understandable that we would be depressed and desperate when undergoing gloomy business. _____ we face the difficulties and kill the rough time is very significant. _____ Helen has gone through may serve as a reminder for each of us.

Guys，from my point of view，_____ ups and downs appear in my life is a process during which I can experience the truth and beauty of life，which is the fascinating insight I comprehend from *Three Days to See*.

【Design intention】For Activity 1, by filling in the blanks cooperatively, students will be provided with the related context to learn the structure of subject clauses effectively. By matching the main idea, students will be attracted by the topic of this class and basically know what is a reading insight. For Activity 2, students are offered a chance to consolidate what they've internalized and digested. Hence, students will be provided with opportunities to learn how to use the subject clauses effectively in an open atmosphere. At the same time they are encouraged to take an active part in the activities. For the Activity 3, by filling in the blanks individually, students will digest the grammar by independent thinking and know how to write a speech of a reading insight.

Step 4. Practice: Read a conclusion speech and do an interview.

Activity. Work in pairs : Fill in the blanks and do an interview.

Morning, guys,

It's an honor _____ I can share my insights from reading with you. It's said _____ reading makes a full man. _____ I'd like to share is that reading has absolutely changed my life experiences.

Intellectually, _____ shapes my mind most is undoubtedly from reading books. Accordingly, _____ sticks in my mind results in what reflects in my action. Consequently, _____ I have read through has illustrated how the emergence of a talented young man comes into being, which is the reason why I am standing here sharing my sensibility upon reading with you. It is self-evident that reading is the easiest shortcut to fulfil my dream. Without reading, I'm definitely nobody.

As Francis Bacon said, "Study serves for delight, for ornament and for ability". Nevertheless, it is widely recognized _____ reading is the basic step for study. Therefore, _____ can be concluded is that reading plays an indispensable part for delight, for ornament and for ability.

Pair work: Recite the speech again and do the interview.

(student A and student B take turns to act as the Speaker and the Host.)

An interview:

Host: Welcome to our Reading Seminar. May I ask you some questions?

Speaker: Sure.

Host: So what would you like to share?

Speaker: ...

Host: What shapes your mind most?

Speaker: ...

Host: What is self-evident for you?

Speaker: ...

Host: Thanks for your sharing.

Attention:

The students who answer the questions should use the subject clauses.

【Design intention】By filling in the blanks in pairs, students will be provided with the related context to check if they really know the structures of subject clauses and then internalize the grammar themselves. By performing the interview, students are offered a chance to consolidate what they've internalized. At the same time they are inspired to think about their own inner thoughts, thus arousing their desire to share their insights and read more books.

Step 5. Writing.

If you are given a chance to deliver a speech concerning the reading insight, please compose a reading insight speech.

Attention:

1. Please try to use subject clauses as many as possible.

2. Every correct subject clause is worth 10 points.

【Design intention】This part is designed to help students to put what they have learned into practical use. Meanwhile, students are expected to express themselves in English correctly by using the grammar, which is indispensable for them to form an English thinking mode and understand the difference between Chinese and English better.

Step 6. Presentation.

Two students are invited to share their speeches concerning the reading insight.

Step 7. Homework.

1. Polish your speech especially where there is any mistake.

2. Read your speech to your friends.

教学设计四——亲子陪伴

Step 1. To be an observer.

Please analyse a sentence and find out the subject and predicative clauses.

From Unit 3，we know money can not buy everything，but money is very important. For us students，we need money to pay school fees. It is our parents who make money to ensure our education. So：

What I want to know is whether you have ever asked how much money your father or mother earns each month/each day/an hour.

【Design intention】A sentence is used to stimulate students' thinking and get them to analyse the structure of the sentence，making students have a preliminary understanding of the subject clauses and the predicative clauses.

Step 2. To be a reader.

There is a story about a little boy who wants to know how much his daddy makes an hour，so let's enjoy the story. Please read the passage and finish the comprehending exercises.

Daddy，how much do you make an hour？

A man came home from work late，tired and irritated，to find his 5-year-old son waiting for him at the door.

"Daddy，may I ask you a question？"

"Yeah，sure，what is it？" replied the man.

"Daddy，how much do you make an hour？"

"If you must know，I make 20 dollars an hour."

"Oh," the little boy replied，with his head down.

Looking up，he said，"Daddy，may I please borrow 10 dollars？"

The father was very angry, "If the only reason why you asked that is that you can borrow some money to buy a silly toy, then you march yourself straight to your room and go to bed."

The little boy quietly went to his room and shut the door. The man sat down and started to get even angrier about the boy's questions.

After about an hour or so, the man had calmed down, and went to the door of the little boy's room and opened it.

"I've been thinking, maybe I was too hard on you earlier, " said the man, "here's the 10 dollars you asked for."

The little boy sat straight up, smiling, "Oh, thank you Daddy! " he yelled.

Then, reaching under his pillow he pulled out some crumpled up bills.

"Why do you want more money if you already have some? " the father said.

"Because I didn't have enough, but now I do." the little boy replied.

"Daddy, I have 20 dollars now. Can I buy an hour of your time? Please come home early tomorrow. I would like to have dinner with you."

The father put his arms around his little son, and begged for his forgiveness.

After reading, finish the following passage in pairs using the subject clauses and predicative clauses.

The little boy was waiting at the door. That is because _____ when his father came back. He asked his father three questions. _____ is his first one. _____ is his second one. _____ is his third one. _____ （让他父亲迷惑的是）was _____ （他向他爸爸借十美元）. What he really wanted was that _____ （他想买他爸爸的一小时，以便于第二天跟他一起用餐）. _____（父亲意识到）was _____（他很少陪伴儿子）and felt very sorry.

【Design intention】By reading and completing the passage, students are encouraged to find out the answers using clauses based on their understanding of the story. While checking the answers, the teacher will guide them to summarize the rules of the grammar.

Step 3. To be a speaker.

There is a popular sentence on the Internet: Put down the work, but I can not support you. Take up the work, but I can not accompany you. The sentence expresses the bitterness of countless parents. So what's your opinion? Try to use the subject clauses and predictive clauses to express your ideas.

The following sentence patterns may help you:

1. _____ makes me worried/happy/upset is that _____.

2. _____ I think/believe is that _____.

3. _____ we understand our parents depends on _____.

4. The reason why we need/don't need their company is _____.

5. My concern is _____.

6. It seems as if _____.

7. _____ is the most important /the worst is that _____.

8. _____ they want to see is that _____.

9. My idea is _____.

10. It is convenient that _____.

【Design intention】This part aims to help students consolidate subject clauses and predicative clauses by doing the exercises above. Also the teacher can lead students to explore more points related to the grammar based on the exercises.

Step 4. To be a reporter.

Nowadays, many parents don't work and rent apartments near schools to accompany their children. Do we need our parents' company or not? What is your opinion? Give your reasons. Discuss in groups and try to use the subject clauses and predictive clauses to express yourself. Then the teacher chooses three or four groups to report their discussion to the class.

【Design intention】This step aims to help students practise more about the grammar and express themselves clearly and logically as well as using subject clauses and predicative clauses in written English, also give them chances to show themselves, which can build up their confidence.

Step 5. To be a judge.

Ask the students to do peer evaluation on their reports based on the following points.

1. Does the report cover subject clauses and predictive clauses?　　Yes./No.

2. Does the report clearly express their opinions?　　Yes./No.

3. Were the relatives used properly（that, whether/if, who, whom, what, which, whose, where, how, why）?　　Yes./No.

4. Was the report well-organized by using subject clauses and predictive clauses?　　Yes./No.

【Design intention】The purpose of this activity is to give students chances to learn from others, which can give them much help to improve their own writing later.

Step 6. To be a writer.

Finish your passage according to the following requirements and hand it in on time.

1. Properly use the subject clauses and predicative clauses.

2. Continue your passage after the given beginning.

3. Include supportive ideas and disapproving ideas as well as reasons.

Do we need our parents' company or not?

What our class have discussed today is _____

_____

_____

_____

_____

_____

_____.

【Design intention】Writing belongs to the output of language learning. The purpose of this activity is to test how much the students have mastered what they have learned in this period, and help them consolidate what have been learned in the class better.

The sample by the teacher:

What our class have discussed today is whether students should be accompanied by parents studying at school. Opinions are divided on the topic.

Most of my classmates hold a view that there is no need for parents to do so. One reason is that we may fall into the habit of dependence, which will have a bad effect on our overall development. The other is that our parents' company can make it hard for us to develop our self-control ability.

However, the others are in favor of it. In their opinion, with parents accompanying us, we can spare more time to concentrate on our study and we will become healthier. What our parents really want to see is that we can overcome difficulties on our own with their encouragement and develop a good habit of studying.

第三节　名词性从句作同位语

教学设计一——动物保护

Step 1. Lead-in: Two heart-broken videos and comments.

Please watch the two videos and listen to comments from netizens.

The first video: Save the Polar Bear.

Comments:

1. Mark: The fact that the globe is becoming warmer and warmer should be valued.

2. Henry: I have the suggestion that relevant departments should take effective measures as soon as possible.

3. Gary: I have no idea whether the bear will survive.

4. Bill: I hold the opinion that nothing is more important than protecting the environment.

The second video: Our Planet.

Comments：

1. Martin：The fact that the walruses climbed up there shocked me.

2. William：I have no idea why the walruses jumped off the cliff.

3. Joseph：There is no doubt that we should spare no effort to protect the environment to fight against the global warming.

4. Amy：I have the advice that the sense of protecting the environment should be strengthened.

【Design intention】In this part，watching two videos aims to stimulate students' enthusiasm and provide the background of this lesson. The comments below the videos help students know what is the appositive clause and introduce the grammar.

Step 2. Video narrations.

Please read the narrations about the two videos.

The first video narration：

This starving polar bear was spotted by a national geographic photographer Paul Nicklen who was on an adventure in the Baffin Islands. Polar bears lose access to the main source of their diet — seals because of the fact that temperature rises，and glaciers melt. Starving and running out of energy，the bears are forced to wander into human settlements for the purpose that they want to get food. The opinion that polar bears can be fed is wrong according to Animal Welfare Act. Without finding another kind of food，there is some doubt whether the bear will survive，maybe just a few hours to live.

The second video narration：

Walruses have to come to land because of the fact that the sea level is declining. Without the water，there is no doubt that the eyesight of walruses is poor. But they can sense the others down below. As they get hungry，they need to return to the sea. However，it finally becomes an unavoidable fact that they fall off the cliff. The idea that walruses will not die out is obviously a joke.

【Design intention】Step 2 is the reappearance of the language knowledge in Step 1. Students can get the basic structure of the appositive clauses introduced by that，whether，what，who，when，where，why，how，especially that and the modified abstract nouns such as fact, opinion, doubt, suggestion... Besides, from Step 1 to Step 2, students can have a better understanding from the appositive clause to the usage of the appositive clause in the text step by step.

Step 3. Be a designer—brainstorm and talk.

What is your feeling after seeing the two videos and narrations above? If you are expected to make a video to call on more people to protect animals, what kind of points should be involved in your video?

Activity 1. Have brainstorming about the points.

Requirements：

1. The students who expresses ideas must use appositive clauses.

2. You can refer to the information below.

Reference：

1. The fact should be stated.

2. More and more animals are endangered because of the global warming.

3. The suggestion should be reflected.

4. Relevant laws should be made.

Example：

The suggestion that relevant laws should be made can be reflected in the video.

Activity 2. Make a dialogue in pairs.

Example：

S1: I am so glad that you can join us in making the video. What do you think should be reflected in the video?

S2: In my opinion, the truth that more and more animals are endangered for the reason that the globe is becoming warmer and warmer should be reflected.

【Design intention】In this part, students are encouraged to design some points involved in their own videos firstly, in fact, which is a sentence-making exercise. Then, students are expected to make a dialogue, actually, which aims to help students use the language knowledge in communicating and pave the way for the next step.

Step 4. Be a writer.

After your brainstorming and talking about your video, now you are supposed to write a narration of your video to make others know the meaning you want to reflect.

Attention：

1. Please try to use appositive clauses as many as possible.

2. Every correct appositive clause is worth 10 points.

Example：

The truth that the globe is becoming warmer and warmer is known around the world. While it may be not clear for everyone how serious the consequences are, the fact that more and more animals are endangered is worrying. I have the advice that relevant laws should be made. I know maybe someone has no idea what we can do. From saving every drop of water to refusing fur products，the belief that we can do a lot should be built. The opinion that animals will not die out is ridiculous. We all are supposed to make a promise that we will try our best to contribute to the animal protection.

【Design intention】In previous steps，students have had a better understanding about the usage of the appositive clause from sentences to texts. In this step，students are expected to write a narration for their own videos designed in Step 3. Actually，from Step 3 to Step 4，it aims to help students do exercises from sentence making to text writing.

Step 5. Presentation.

Two students share their narrations and others try to help them make some corrections.

Step 6. Homework.

Polish your narration and hand it in on time.

教学设计二——新年祝愿

Step 1. Lead-in：Listen and fill in the blanks.

With the Year of Ox approaching，there is no doubt _____ everything will take on a new look. Though we have gone through ups and downs in the Year of Mouse, I still hold the firm belief _____ there is hope in the new dawn even on the darkest nights. If you ask me the question _____ all the experiences in the Year of Mouse were worth, the answer _____ everything was worth remains as solid as rocks. Would you like to express the hope/wish _____ no matter how high the mountain is, one can always reach its top for the Year of Ox?

【Design intention】The purpose of listening to the clip is to introduce the teaching target—the noun clauses as the appositive in this class. Students are expected to fill in the blanks with related conjunctions such as that and whether introducing the appositive clauses by listening practice.

Step 2. Pair work: Work in pairs to ask and answer the following questions.

1. What kind of regret will make you feel the Year of Mouse unworthy?

The regret that _____ will make me feel the Year of Mouse unworthy.

2. What suggestion will you put forward for fighting against the COVID-19?

I put forward the suggestion that _____.

3. What thought will come to your mind with the Year of Ox coming?

With the Year of Ox coming, the thought comes to my mind that _____.

4. What wish will you express about the Year of Ox?

About the Year of Ox, I express the wish that _____.

【Design intention】By observing and answering the questions, students will have a basic understanding of the appositive clauses introduced by that. During this period, students are encouraged to be familiar with the sentence structure as well.

Step 3. Practice: A turntable game.

Whoever gets a chance to do the turntable game can choose the words at random in the charts below to make sentences or you can choose the words you like by using appositive clauses.

> wish, hope, doubt, thought, news, idea

<table>
<tr><td>opinion, suggestion, belief, fact, request...</td><td>express, make, be, have, represent, ring true, echo back...</td></tr>
</table>

Example：

1. My wish that everything will goes well in the Year of Ox can represent yours.

2. His suggestion that everyone should wear masks still rings true.

3. My request that we can make it possible to defeat the COVID-19 is urgent.

【Design intention】By making sentences, students will be provided with opportunities to learn to use the appositive clauses effectively in an open atmosphere. At the same time they are encouraged to take an active part in the activities.

Step 4. Read the letter, fill in the blanks and answer the questions.

Activity 1. Work in groups： Fill in the blanks to complete the letter.

Dear the Year of Ox,

The saying _____ millions of people are united to overcome the epidemic still rings true in my inner heart. Simultaneously, the statement _____ time and tide wait for no man echoes with tears and laughter through the Year of Mouse. As the Year of Ox is approaching, my wishes _____ my beloved family, my lovely students and my great motherland are going right along are as follows.

Initially, to my beloved family, in line with the belief _____ I will do whatever it takes to serve my family regardless of the fortune and misfortune. This is my only request _____ you should carefully take care of yourselves. Additionally, to my lovely students, there is no doubt _____ you have unforgettable online classes. This is my hope _____ you can spare no efforts to study hard whether you have classes online or offline. The fact _____ the situation of the epidemic is still far from good is known to us. You may have no idea _____ you will be able to get it done in such a long period. Don't panic. Because our great motherland always protects us against any gloomy business. Finally, to my great motherland, though having gone through numerous rough patches, the whole country lights up the sky and guides us in the times ahead. My promise _____ I will maintain by all means

in my power as a qualified citizen will never change. Accordingly, this is my desire
_____ my country will become much more prosperous than ever.

In a word, no matter what it will be in the coming Year of Ox, I hold the firm
belief _____ everything will go as we wish. Let me assure you of my thoughts and
prayers.

Yours,

Anonymity

Activity 2. Pair work: Read the letter again and answer the following questions.

1. What kind of request does Anonymity ask for the beloved family?

2. What hope of the lovely students will you conclude?

3. What desire does Anonymity raise for the great motherland?

Attention: The students who answer the questions should use the appositive
clauses.

【Design intention】For activity 1, by filling in the blanks, students will
be provided with the related context to learn the structure of appositive clauses
effectively. For activity 2, by answering the questions, students are offered a
chance to consolidate what they've internalized and digested. At the same time they
are inspired to think about their own inner thoughts, thus arousing their emotion to
express their wishes for the Year of Ox.

Step 5. Writing.

As the Year of Ox is approaching, there is no doubt that you have much to wish
for your best friends. Please write a letter to your best friends.

Attention:

1. Please try to use appositive clauses as many as possible.

2. Every correct appositive clause is worth 10 points.

【Design intention】This part is designed to help students to put what they have
learned into practical use. Meanwhile, students are expected to express themselves in
English correctly by using the grammar, which is indispensable for them to form an
English thinking mode and understand the differences between Chinese and English
better.

Step **6**. Presentation.

Two students are invited to share their letters with their best wishes to their best friends.

Step **7**. Homework.

Polish your letter and send it to someone whom you wrote to.

教学设计三——手机使用

Step **1**. Lead-in：Question.

The teacher enters the classroom with a cell phone, and asks students to guess why he/she brings a cell phone into the classroom.

Q：Do you know why I bring a cell phone into class?

A：I guess the fact that the teacher brings a cell phone into the classroom is that...

【Design intention】The intention of the question is to arouse students' curiosity, stimulate students' desire to speak their ideas out and help the whole class go on the next step.

Step **2**. Discussion.

The teacher leads into a discussion about the idea whether students can bring their cell phones into school.

Discussion：Do you think whether you can bring your cell phone into school?

A1：Agree.

A2：Disagree.

【Design intention】The purpose of the discussion is to push students to get involved in the activities of the class and think about the questions' and encourage them to express their ideas.

Step **3**. Debate.

According to the discussion above, students will be divided into two groups. One agrees the idea that students can bring cell phones into school, and the other holds the opinion that they cannot.

Possible answers:

Group 1: ① We can use cell phones to search for some useful information.

② We can use cell phones to keep in touch with our parents whenever and wherever.

③ ...

Group 2: ① We cannot focus our attention on study with cell phones.

② Lots of students use cell phones to play games rather than study.

③ ...

【Design intention】In this part, students are expected to cooperate with their team members to form some logical ideas and express themselves bravely. In the meanwhile, students can learn from each other.

Activity. Practice.

1. Fill in the blanks.

(1) We have a question _____.

(学校是否允许学生带手机进学校)

(2) I have some doubt _____.

(父母是否支持我们带手机进学校)

(3) We are all confused about the opinion _____.

(手机是有利于还是有害于我们的学习)

2. Ask the representative of each group to write their opinions down on the blackboard.

(1) We will have a debate on the idea whether students can bring their cell phones into school. (An example from the teacher)

(2) We hold the opinion that students can bring cell phones into school.

(3) We hold the belief that students can use cell phones to search for some useful information.

(4) We believe the fact that using a cell phone can make students keep in touch with their parents whenever and wherever they want to.

(5) I agree with the idea that we should not bring cell phones into school.

(6) We support the idea that the cell phones are harmful to students.

（7）The students can't keep the promise that they will spend more time on study rather than entertainments.

【Design intention】In this activity, students are supposed to experience the usage of the appositive clauses and focus on the conjunctions to understand and feel the rules of appositive clauses. The activities can help them come to understand the basic structure of the noun clauses as the appositive introduced by that and whether.

Step 4. Writing.

Ask the students to write a composition to summarize the process of the class and their own attitudes towards the topic using appositive clauses as many as possible.

At the beginning of the class, our English teacher entered the classroom with a cell phone, and the teacher told us that we would have a debate on the idea whether students could bring their cell phones into school.

Some students hold the opinion that students can bring cell phones into school. They hold the belief that they would use cell phones to search for some useful information as well as keep in touch with their parents whenever and wherever they want to. However, others are for the idea that cell phones are harmful to students. They can't keep their promise that they will spend more time on study rather than entertainments. As far as I am concerned, I agree the view that we should not bring cell phones into school.

Finally, the teacher drew a conclusion that both views are reasonable as long as we use the cell phone wisely/properly.

【Design intention】By writing a composition, the students can not only review what they have learned in this class, but also have a chance to organize their ideas, which can practice their thinking ability and writing ability.

Step 5. Homework.

Polish your summary and exchange it with your deskmate to help each other.

教学设计四——师生友谊

Step 1. Listen and fill：Enjoy *As Long as You Love Me* and try to fill in the blanks.

Don't care _____ is written in your history, as long as you're here with me.

I don't care _____ you are, _____ you're from, _____ you did.

...

Don't care _____ you did, as long as you love me.

Every little thing that you've said and done,

Feels like it's deep within me.

Doesn't really matter _____ you're on the run.

【Design intention】A beautiful song is played to the class to arouse students' learning interest and at the same time to introduce the target —noun clauses in this class.

Step 2. True or false：Do the following sentences belong to noun clauses? Which ones belong to noun clauses? And what type are they?

1. We hope that you will accept our invitation at your most convenient time. (   )

2. The students who are going to take these courses have at least three years of English learning experiences. (   )

3. His suggestion is that we should read more relevant books to collect more information about Chinese knots. (   )

4. There was once a folk custom that married daughters ought not to do any cleaning in their mothers' home. (   )

5. Whatever she wants，her parents try every means to meet her demands. (   )

6. What you have done in the voluntary work has made a great difference for our environmental protection. (   )

【Design intention】By analyzing these sentences，some basic knowledge about noun clauses can be effectively reviewed and refreshed. And also the exercises can lay a good foundation of the following part — language focus.

Step **3**. Language focus：Choose a proper conjunction to fill in the blank.

1. if / whether

（1）I asked her _____ she had a bike.

（2）We didn't know _____ she was ready or not.

（3）We're worried about _____ he is safe.

（4）The question is _____ the film is worth seeing.

（5）I have no idea _____ I can pass this driving test.

（6）_____ he can come to the party on time depends on the traffic.

2. whether/that

（1）I doubt _____ he can speak English.

（2）I don't doubt _____ he can speak English.

（3）There is little doubt _____ he can speak English.

（4）There is some doubt _____ he can speak English.

3. that/what

（1）The news is _____ we won the competition.

（2）His father is satisfied with _____ he has done.

（3）China is not _____ it used to be.

（4）We live in _____ is called "the Information Age".

（5）After _____ seemed several hours，she finally came to life.

（6）The reason was _____ Tom had never seen the million pound bank note.

4. what/whatever；who/whoever

（1）_____ you said moved me a great deal.

（2）Parents can't give their children _____ they want.

（3）_____ breaks the law will be punished.

（4）_____ robbed the bank is not clear.

5. why/because

（1）He was late for school this morning. That's _____ he got up late.

（2）He got up late. That's _____ he was late for school this morning.

【Design intention】 These conjunctions are the most difficult part in noun clauses. This is where most of the students often make mistakes. By comparison, it is easier for students to understand the differences between them so that they can use noun clauses in specific contexts more effectively.

Step 4. Read and fill: Please read the following letter and make it complete by using the proper conjunctions.

Dear students,

How time flies! The National Entrance Examination is just around the corner. To be frank, I can't fall fast asleep recently because of anxiety disorder（焦虑症）. _____ makes me awake is _____ I'm always worried about the efficiency of online courses. Of course, another reason is _____ I don't want to say goodbye to you because of your graduating from our school.

Actually, the days we spent together are full of joys and tears. _____ you were always careless used to make me annoyed. However, I'm always here to give my hand to _____ turns to me for help.

Now I understand _____ we have experienced together is of great value to me. Actually, don't care too much about _____ you can make your dream come true or not. Because _____ you should cherish（珍惜）most is _____ you have enjoyed the process of struggling. Please remember: the harder you work, the luckier you will be. I sincerely wish _____ all of you would be admitted to your dream universities in the coming year.

Best wishes!

Yours,

Zhang Li

【Design intention】 This letter is designed to check if students have achieved the main learning goal of this class and help students to use noun clauses in specific contexts correctly, which is also beneficial to the language output of their own in the following step.

Step 5. Write a letter to give Miss Zhang some advice to help relieve anxiety with the help of the following structure.

Para. 1. The purpose of writing this letter.

Para. 2. Your suggestions.

Para. 3. Best wishes.

Attention：

1. Please try to use noun clauses as many as possible.

2. Every correct noun clause is worth 10 points.

Dear Miss. Zhang，

_____

_____

_____

_____

_____

_____

_____

Yours sincerely，

Li Hua

【Design intention】In this part，students are required to write a letter to give their teacher some advice to help her relieve anxiety by using as many noun clauses as possible，which not only can consolidate what they have reviewed in this class but also develop their awareness of taking care of others so that they can have a good relationship with others in daily life.

Step 6. Sharing time.

Invite two or three students to share their advice given to Miss Zhang.

Step 7. Homework.

Polish your letter and make sure your suggestions are practical and useful.

第三章

时态和语态教学设计

第一节　现在进行时表示将来

教学设计一——个人旅行计划

Step 1. Show students some pictures about Hainan.

【Design intention】The pictures are about the beautiful scenery of Hainan, which can show students the topic about this grammar learning class. Besides, it aims to stimulate students' enthusiasm in this class.

Step 2. Read the travel plan and answer the questions.

As the vacation is coming, I am travelling to Hainan, a place full of sunshine. Considering plane is the quickest and the most comfortable, I am flying there. I am leaving on December 3rd and I am coming back on December 10th. When I arrive there, I am staying in a hotel near the beach so that I can walk along the beach and feel the quietness and power of the sea. Before leaving, I am buying some necessities such as sunglasses, sun cream and so on. I think I will have a pleasant time.

1. Where is Miss Liu travelling?

2. How is Miss Liu going there?

3. What is Miss Liu going to do about her travel? Please underline the answers

in her travel plan.

【Design intention】In this part, students need to read the travel plan first and then answer the questions, which can help students experience the target grammar in this class.

Step 3. Listen and fill in the blanks.

As the vacation is coming, I am _____ to Hainan, a place full of sunshine. Considering plane is the quickest and the most comfortable, I am _____ there. I am on December 3rd and I am _____ back on December 10th. When I arrive there, I am _____ in a hotel near the beach so that I can walk along the beach and feel the quietness and power of the sea. Before leaving, I am _____ some necessities such as sunglasses, sun cream and so on. I think I will have a pleasant time.

【Design intention】In this part, students are expected to fill in the blanks by using present continuous tense to express future actions while listening.

Step 4. Retell Miss Liu's travel plan.

Be sure to use as many sentences using the present continuous tense to express the future actions as possible.

【Design intention】Students are given some pictures about Hainan first and then they need to retell the travel plan according to the given pictures, which can help students to retell the travel plan by using present continuous tense to express future actions.

Step 5. Make a dialogue.

1. Brainstorm something that you want to do during your holiday.

2. Work in groups of six to make a dialogue with your deskmate to know what he/she is doing in his/her holiday. You can begin your dialogue like this:

Y: Hi! The five-day holiday is coming, and I feel excited. What are you doing on the first day of your holiday?

D: Let me think. Oh, I am watching a movie with my parents.

Y: Wow. That sounds great. What are you doing the second day of your holiday?

D: ...

【Design intention】The dialogue can enable students to talk about their own travel plans by using present continuous tense to express the future actions.

Step 6. Write down your own travel plan.

Be sure to use as many sentences using present continuous tense to express the future actions as possible.

【Design intention】In this part, students are expected to write down their own travel plan by using as many sentences including present continuous tense to express the future actions as possible.

教学设计二——班级出游计划

Step 1. Lead-in: Listen and fill.

Good evening, everyone. As the beautiful summer＿＿＿＿（come）, we ＿＿＿＿（go）to launch a whole-class summer travel in the coming mid-July. During this class, everyone is expected to talk about the travel plan, which includes where we ＿＿＿＿（go）, when we＿＿＿＿（set）off and＿＿＿＿（arrive）, how we ＿＿＿＿（get）there and why we＿＿＿＿（travel）there. Your participation and suggestions will play an important role in the final plan.

【Design intention】The purpose of listening to the clip is to introduce the teaching target —present continuous tense expressing futurity in this class. Students are expected to fill in the blanks with "be doing" introducing present continuous tense expressing futurity.

Step 2. Pair work: Ask and answer.

1. Why are we going to launch a summer travel?

2. What should be included in your travel plan?

【Design intention】By observing and answering the questions, students will have a basic understanding of present continuous tense expressing futurity. During this stage, students are encouraged to be familiar with the structure as well.

Step 3. Discuss and share, and then read and fill.

Activity 1. Discuss your travel plan in your group and share it with us.

Please try your best to clarify the following points：

P1： Where are we going?

We are going...

P2： When are we leaving and arriving?

We are leaving on... and arriving on...

P3： How are we getting the destination?

We are getting there by...

P4： Why are we travelling there?

The reason why we are travelling there is that...

Activity 2. Read the following speech and fill in the blanks individually.

Good morning， dear boys and girls. As your English teacher， I am also tremendously expecting the whole-class summer travel. Your comprehensive consideration and conducive suggestions are definitely indispensable for our travel plan. Simultaneously， I'd like to offer the following tips.

To begin with， when we _____ （travel） to other places， be sure to behave ourselves， for example， avoiding shouting and respecting local customs. In addition， since it is a whole-class activity， no matter where we _____ （go） and when we _____ （arrive） , we are supposed to follow the class rules. Last but not the least， before we _____ （leave） for the destination， it is necessary for us to make good preparations such as the sun-proof clothing and mosquito-proof spray.

In conclusion， the whole-class summer travel is a meaningful activity for us to relax ourselves and broaden our horizons. Before we _____ （leave） , we are bound to make good preparations. After we _____ （arrive） there， we are expected to be civilized travelers. Hope all of us enjoy the coming travel.

【Design intention】For the activity 1， by discussing the travelling plan cooperatively， students will be provided the related context to learn the structure and usage of the present continuous tense expressing futurity effectively. Meanwhile， students are offered a chance to consolidate what they've internalized and digested.

Hence, students will be provided opportunities to learn how to use the structure effectively in an open atmosphere. At the same time they are encouraged to take an active part in the activities. For the activity 2, by filling in the blanks individually, students will digest the grammar by independent thinking. Simultaneously, students are cultivated to be those who can follow collective rules and behave as civilized travelers, which also offers a stage for students to be qualified citizens through learning English.

Step 4. Writing.

If you were the monitor, after listening to the stated suggestions, you would deliver a conclusion speech about the whole-class summer travel plan.

Attention:

1. Please try to use sentences including present continuous tense expressing futurity as many as possible.

2. Every correct sentence using present continuous tense expressing futurity is worth 10 points.

【 Design intention 】 This part is designed to help students to put what they have learned into practical use. Meanwhile, students are expected to express themselves in English correctly by using the grammar, which is indispensable for them to form an English thinking mode and understand the difference between Chinese and English better.

Step 5. Presentation.

Two students are invited to share their conclusion speech and others try to make some comments about it.

Step 6. Homework.

Polish your conclusion speech and hand it in on time.

第二节　一般将来时的被动语态

教学设计一——家长会

Step 1. Lead-in：Listen and fill in the blanks.

Good afternoon, honorable headmaster and parents, dear teachers and students. Welcome to this parents' meeting.

What will _____ (do) in this meeting is to discuss what measures will _____ (take) to tremendously better the current situation. Any suggestion or measure related to this important issue _____ (welcome). Three parts _____ (include) in this meeting, that is, a speech _____ (deliver) by a representative parent, and measures concerning home-school cooperation _____ (explain) by Mr. Liu, our teacher-in-chief and suggestions _____ (put forward) by a representative student. Let's proceed with them one by one.

【Design intention】The purpose of listening to the clip is to introduce the teaching target—future passive voice in this class. Students are expected to fill in the blanks with "will be done" introducing future passive voice.

Step 2. Pair work：Work in pairs to ask and answer the following questions.

1. What will be done in this meeting?

2. Will any suggestions be welcomed?

3. How many parts will be included?

【Design intention】By observing and answering the questions, students will have a basic understanding of the future passive voice. During this period, students are encouraged to be familiar with the structure as well.

Step 3. Read and fill, and then discuss and share.

Activity 1. Read the speech and fill in the blanks in groups.

Honorable headmaster and teachers, dear students,

Delighted to hear effective measures＿＿＿＿（take）in the coming days. The following aspects＿＿＿＿（put）into use later and also it is the suggestions that＿＿＿＿（share）with you.

To begin with, more attention＿＿＿＿（pay）to kids' overall development but not the examination result only than ever before. In addition, during the following days intensive supervision＿＿＿＿（not put）on kids because they can't hold overwhelmingly parental attention. Last but not the least, the saying to be treated equally by elders＿＿＿＿（fulfil）as promised in the coming days. Simultaneously, hope home-school cooperation＿＿＿＿（launch）more effectively as well as parents' initiative＿＿＿＿（arouse）through a wide range of measures.

In a nutshell, it is only with practical actions that we can ensure upward growth and development. I hold the firm belief that great progress＿＿＿＿（make）by our united resolution and actions next three months.

Activity 2. Free talk（pair work）.

If you were parents, would you please come up with more suggestions or measures to help develop students' health both mentally and physically using one or two future passive voice?

Eg 1: home-school cooperation ——➤ hold more

Home-school cooperation will be held more.

Eg 2: students' outdoor activities ——➤ organize more

Eg 3: students' daily behavior ——➤ communicate in details

Eg 4: food in student's canteen ——➤ diversify

Eg 5: education-related facilities ——➤ advance

Eg 6: students' academic results ——➤ analyse objectively and scientifically

Activity 3. Speaking.

Share your suggestions with the whole class.

Attention:

Please use the future passive voice.

【Design intention】For the activity 1, by filling in the blanks cooperatively, students will be provided the related context to learn the structure and usage of the future passive voice effectively. For the activity 2, students are offered a chance to consolidate what they've internalized and digested. For the activity 3, students will be given a chance to put what they've learned into practical use. Hence, students will be provided opportunities to learn how to use the future passive voice effectively in an open atmosphere. At the same time they are encouraged to take an active part in the activities.

Step 4. Practice: Read another speech and do an interview.

Activity. Fill in the blanks individually and do an interview in groups.

Honorable parents,

Thanks for your suggestions and actions. As is recognized, in the coming days, from the perspective of parents, delicate consideration_____ (give) to students. Apart from what has been mentioned above, dear parents, from my point of view, I do hope that the following three aspects _____ (put) into practice by you as well.

Primarily, during next three months, more conducive and necessary participation _____ (welcome) to effectively enhance home-school cooperation. Additionally, in the near future, adequate understanding and objective comments _____ (need) to create a harmonious and fair atmosphere instead of complaint and criticism. Ultimately, excessive interference _____ (not accept) during the following three months since education is actually a professional issue.

Undoubtedly, since home-school cooperation refers to the cooperation between home and school, there is no denying that the utmost efforts_____ (put) into all students overall development and growth from the aspect of our school. In a word, the same goal _____ (maintain) in the coming days with you all, that is, hope each of students _____ (admit) into their longing universities three months later with the joint triple efforts.

Pair work: Recite the speech again and do the interview.

(Student A and Student B take turns to act as the Speaker and the Host.)

An interview：

Host：Mr. Liu，thanks for your speech. May I ask you two questions？

Mr. Liu：Sure.

Host：So from your point of view，what will be done by parents ？

Mr. Liu：...

Host：What is your same goal?

Mr. Liu：...

Host：Thanks for your sharing.

Attention：

The students who act as Mr. Liu should use the future passive voice.

【Design intention】By filling in the blanks individually，students will be provided the related context to check if they really know the structures of the future passive voice and then internalize the grammar themselves. By performing the interview，students are offered a chance to consolidate what they've internalized. At the same time they are inspired to think about their own inner thoughts，thus arousing their desire to share their ideas about what measures will be taken to better themselves.

Step 5. Writing.

As a representative student，if you are given a chance to deliver a speech concerning what measures will be taken to better the current situation，there is no doubt that you have much to express. Please compose the speech.

Attention：

1. Please try to use future passive voice as much as possible.

2. Every correct future passive voice is worth 10 points.

【Design intention】This part is designed to help students to put what they have learned into practical use. Meanwhile，students are expected to express themselves in English correctly by using the grammar，which is indispensable for them to form an English thinking mode and understand the difference between Chinese and English better.

Step **6**. Presentation.

Two students are invited to share their speech about how to improve the current situation while others should listen carefully and try to give more practical suggestions.

Step 7. Homework.

Polish your speech by adding more useful advice according to the specific situation in your class and read it to your headteacher to create a better class atmosphere.

教学设计二——冬奥会

Step **1**. Lead-in：A guessing game.

1. The 24th Winter Olympic Games <u>will be held</u> in 2022.

2. The 24th Winter Olympic Games <u>will be hosted</u> in two cities of a country.

3. The winners in the 24th Winter Olympic Games <u>will be awarded</u> medals.

【Design intention】A guessing game is used to introduce the teaching aim in this class and arouse students' interest.

Step **2**. Listen and fill in the following blanks.

The 24th Winter Olympic Games _____ in two cities of a country.

Many things _____ for the games. Several billion yuan _____ on the projects. And a special village _____ for the athletes and some hotels _____ for the visitors to stay in. The road _____ wider and better and trees and flowers _____ along the roads. The new stadium _____ before 2022. Many volunteers _____ for the Games. Many policemen _____ to keep order.

The 24th Winter Olympic Games _____ a success.

Step **3**. Check answers and summarize the structure of these underlined words.

The 24th Winter Olympic Games <u>will be held</u> in two cities of a country.

Many things <u>will be done</u> for the games. Several billion yuan <u>will be spent</u> on the projects. And a special village <u>is going to be built</u> for the athletes and some hotels

121

will be set up for the visitors to stay in. The road will be made wider and better and trees and flowers will be planted along the roads. The new stadium is to be completed before 2022. Many volunteers will be trained for the Games. Many policemen will be sent to keep order.

The 24th Winter Olympic Games will be made a success.

Structures：

1. _____

2. _____

3. _____

【Design intention】In this part，students will have a basic understanding of future passive voice and then they will have the ability to conclude structure of the future passive voice.

Step 4. Practice.

Activity 1. Make an interview.

Suppose you are Li Hua and the Ankang Sports Meeting will be held next year. Now，you are going to interview the designer of the Ankang Sports Meeting. Work in groups and make interviews with your partners by using the future passive voice. You can refer to the information in the following chart.

roads	clean
athletes	choose
winners	award
volunteers	train
flowers and trees	plant
hotels	order
...	...

Requirements：

1. Every student must make an interview by using the future passive voice.

2. Each pair needs to make at least six sentences.

Example：

Li：Where will all the athletes live?

Designer： All the athletes will be housed in hotels which are near to competition area.

Li： That's great! And how about the roads?

Designer： All the roads in our city will be cleaned and some will be made wider and better.

...

Activity 2. Make interviews in the class.

Every group picks out two students to make an interview and the teacher needs to evaluate them.

【Design intention】Through making up sentences by using the future passive voice, students will be given a chance to consolidate what they have learned. At the same time, when they discuss with their group members, new ideas will come up and they can share their thoughts.

Step 5. Writing.

If the leader of Ankang government sends an e-mail to you to invite you to make a plan for the next An Kang Sports Meeting, please try to make a reply to him.

Attention：

Please try to use future passive voice as much as possible.

Dear leader,

I'm more than glad to receive your e-mail and it's my great honour to shoulder this task. Here is my plan for the Ankang Sports Meeting.

_____

_____

_____

_____

_____.

I hope that you will like it. At the same time, I hope you can give me some suggestions.

Yours,

Li Hua

【Design intention】The purpose of this writing is to give the students another chance to help them consolidate what they have learned in this class. At the same time，students can use the future passive voice to describe the things which will happen in our life.

Step 6. Presentation.

Two students are invited to share their plans and others try to polish them.

Step 7. Homework.

Polish your plan for the next An Kang Sports Meeting and try to exchange it with one of your friends.

第三节　现在完成时的被动语态

教学设计一——亲子关系

Step 1. Lead-in：Read an ancient Chinese poem and answer questions.

Traveler's Song

Sewing threads in my kind mother's hand

was shuttling through a coat for me a wayward boy.

She sewed them before seeing me off neatly closed

for fearing that I might return much too late.

Oh，what can I offer

to repay my kind mother's love?

【Design intention】The topic is introduced by this poem which shows a mother's great love. It also leads students to think about their parents'love and what they have done for them as well as how they should repay their parents.

Step 2. A switching game.

Work in pairs. One student says one nice thing he or she has done for his or her parents. The other one should retell it using "have/has been done".Then they exchange their roles.

Examples：

I have bought a T-shirt for my father.

A T-shirt has been bought for my father.

【Design intention】The purpose of this game is to let students go over the present perfect tense and then observe that it can be transferred to the present perfect passive voice so that they can eventually understand how it is transferred and then put it into practical use.

Step 3. Rewrite the passage about a mother's problems.

I am facing some problems. My boss has given me a lot more work which I can hardly deal with.What's worse，I haven't arranged my daughter Mary's birthday party. My husband can't offer any help because his boss has sent him to Xi'an on a business trip.

I am facing some problems. A lot more work _____ to me，which I can hardly deal with. What's worse，my daughter Mary's birthday party _____. My husband can't offer any help because he _____ to Xi'an on a business trip.

【Design intention】In this part，students are expected to rewrite the passage using the present perfect passive voice，which helps them to practice the proper usage of this target grammar. What's more，it also reminds them that their parents could be in a similar situation.

Step 4. Group discussion.

Imagining you are Mary，try to find out some solutions to help her mother. You are expected to rewrite the first two possible solutions by using the structure of "have/has been done". Then try to write some more solutions using the same structure.

【Design intention】In this step，students are supposed to firstly rewrite the first two solutions using the present perfect passive voice and then try to find out more solutions to Mary's mother's problems. This rewriting and finding activity assists students in improving their creative thinking and mastering the usage of the present perfect passive voice.

Step 5. Write a heart–warming note to Mary's mother.

Imagine you are Mary and please write a heart-warming note to tell her mother some nice things which have been done for her.

【Design intention】This step aims to enhance students' creative thinking and writing ability in a real-life situation using the target grammar learned in this class.

Step 6. Write a heart–warming note to your own parents.

Parents are always concerned about us and eager to know what we are doing at school. Write a heart-warming note to your parents to share your school life this week. It is necessary for you to use "have/has been done". Then you can make a phone call to your parents, expressing your feelings to them.

【Design intention】In another perspective, students will be given a good opportunity to use what they have learned to write a heart-warming note to communicate with their parents, which not only contributes to learning through use but also improves their relationship with their parents.

Step 7. Sharing time.

Invite two students to share their notes with us and others help to polish it at the same time.

【Design intention】In this part, the confidence of the students who are invited to share will be built up, and at the same time the rest of the students will benefit from listening. What's more, the comments from peers and the teacher can help students of different levels.

Step 8. Homework.

Polish the note according to the comments from your classmates and the teacher.

【Design intention】Homework is used to help students consolidate what they have learned in this class so that they can use the present perfect passive voice in their oral and written English effectively.

教学设计二——家乡变化

Step 1. Lead-in：Ask and answer.

Do you remember that President Xi visited Ankang Last year?

Where did he go？And why did he go to Lao Xian at Ping Li for a visit？

Have your hometown changed in the past few years?

【Design intention】The visit of Xi Jinping to Ankang and the related questions are used to introduce the teaching target in this class and arouse students' interest as well.

Step 2. Read and observe：Read what President Xi said when he visited Lao Xian.

I am delighted to see how much Lao Xian has been changed in the past few years. The hospitals and schools have been rebuilt already. Besides, the local factories have been set up and managed very well over the years. It's really good to see that your lives have been greatly changed up to now. Try harder to make it a better place for people to live in. Best wishes to all of you！

【Design intention】In this part, students will have a basic understanding of the present perfect passive voice through observation and discovery, and then they will have the ability to conclude basic rules of the present perfect passive voice.

Step 3. Practice：Talk about the great changes in the teacher's hometown and the students' hometown.

Activity 1. Listen and fill：Listen to the teacher to talk about the great changes in his/her hometown and then fill in the blanks according to the listening text.

My hometown has been greatly changed in the past few years.

Firstly, thousands of trees _____ all over my hometown over the years. Secondly, the schools in my hometown _____ recently in order to give the local children a better education. Thirdly, the hospitals _____ so as to meet the people's needs in the last few years. Fourthly, some factories _____ already and many local people _____ jobs by them up to now. Finally, people's lives _____ by the efforts of the government so far.

Requirements：

1. The students need to focus on the listening and fill in the blanks.

2. The students need to answer what has been done to the trees，the schools，the hospitals，the factories and people's lives in the teacher's hometown.

Example：

Thousands of trees have been planted all over my hometown over the years.

The schools in my hometown have been rebuilt recently in order to give the local children a better education.

The hospitals have been expanded so as to meet the people's needs in the last few years.

【Design intention】In this part，students will focus on listening to the teacher to talk about how his/her hometown has been greatly changed in the past few years. And exercises，filling in the blanks，will help students to think how to use the present perfect passive voice through listening and filling.

Activity 2. Fill in the blanks and do a role-play.

Here is a dialogue between Student A and Student B and then do a role-play.

A：Have you ever been told the great changes in our hometown?

B：It's a pity that I haven't been told about it yet.

A：In the last few years，thousands of trees _____ all over our hometown. Some industries have been set up already.

B：Wow，therefore，many people _____ jobs by the local newly-built industries up to now. Is that so?

A：That's correct! The schools in our hometown _____ recently in order to give the local children a better education.

B：That's really amazing! What about the hospitals?

A：The hospitals _____ so as to meet the people's needs over the years.

B：I feel really happy to be informed the good news. People's lives _____ by the efforts of the government so far.

【Design intention】In this part，students will try to use the present perfect passive voice through filling, and role-playing and then they will better understand how to use the present perfect passive voice by individual learning and cooperative learning.

Activity 3. Discuss with your group members about the great changes in your hometown by using the present perfect passive voice.

Every group leader speaks out the great changes in his/her hometown from different aspects.

Example：

My hometown has been greatly changed over the years. On the one hand， a number of trees have been planted all over my hometown in the last few years. On the other hand， many tall buildings have been set up， which makes my hometown very beautiful.

【Design intention】By talking about the great changes in their hometown， students will be provided opportunities to learn the present perfect passive voice effectively in an open and happy atmosphere. At the same time they are encouraged to take an active part in the activities. "Practice makes perfect." Therefore， through practice， students can better understand how to use the present perfect passive voice.

Step 4. Writing.

Write a letter to Premier Li Keqiang to tell him the great changes in your hometown based on what we have talked about in this class and invite him to Ankang to see how your hometown has been greatly changed over the years.

Attention：

1. Please try to use "have/has been done" as much as possible.

2. Every correct present perfect passive voice sentence is worth 10 points.

Step 5. Presentation.

Two students will be invited to share their letters and others will try to make some comments and also benefit from listening carefully.

Step 6. Homework.

Polish your letter according to the comments given by your classmates and teacher.

教学设计三——感动中国

Step 1. Lead-in： Listen and fill in the blanks.

Good evening, everyone is welcomed to watch CCTV-1 whether on the spot or not. This is Touching China 2020. Let me introduce a modern heroine to you. Over the past twelve years, 111,000 miles of rough path_____ (finish) by her. During these difficult periods, 1804 girls_____ (admit) to universities with her assistance. Since 2008, most of her energy_____ (devote) to the under-privileged area education though her physical condition fell into a terrible state. Thousands of pills _____ (take) by her to fight against illnesses and pains in the past decade. Since 2008, she _____ (respect) by her students, parents and all of us. Let us welcome Mrs. Zhang Guimei with the sincerest applause.

【Design intention】The purpose of listening to the clip is to introduce the teaching target —present perfect passive voice in this class. Students are expected to fill in the blanks with "have/has been done" introducing the present perfect passive voice.

Step 2. Pair work： Work in pairs to ask and answer the following questions.

1. Why is Mrs. Zhang nominated/chosen as a member of Touching China 2020?

2. How did she fight against illnesses and pains ?

3. Can you share what has been done by Mrs. Zhang over the years?

【Design intention】By observing and answering the questions, students will have a basic understanding of the present perfect passive voice. During this stage, students are encouraged to be familiar with the structure as well.

Step 3. Read and fill.

Activity 1. Read the dialogue and fill in the blanks and then do a role-play in groups.

The Reporter: Nice to meet you. I'm a reporter from CCTV-1. Learning that you are one of the students educated and sponsored by Mrs. Zhang, I'm wondering if you can share the story between you and the great modern heroine.

The Student：Sure. Had not assisted by dear Mrs. Zhang，I would not have been given a chance to study. Since 2016，I，as well as my classmates _____ （educate） by our dear Mom，Mrs. Zhang without offering educational fees. Up to now，many girls like me _____ （sponsor） by her. As far as I know，since several years ago，many medical treatments _____ （apply） to Mrs. Zhang. Hope our dear Mom can look after herself not only us.

The Reporter：Thanks for your sharing. I hope so.

Activity 2. Read the other dialogue and fill in the blanks, and then do a role-play in groups.

The Reporter：Glad to see you. I'm a reporter from CCTV-1. Learning that you are one of the girls'parents helped by Mrs. Zhang，I'm wondering if you can share the story between your family and the great modern heroine.

The Parent：My pleasure. Since ten years ago，our three girls_____ （help） by Mrs. Zhang Guimei to have access to education. Actually，till now，many parents like us _____ （offer） the chance to know that girls own the equal right and ability to receive education. Thanks to her devotion and contribution，more attention _____ （pay） to girls'education from the perspective of parents.

The Reporter：Thanks for your sharing. Hope all parents can realize that.

Activity 3. Read a speech and fill in the blanks individually.

Honorable headmasters and teachers，

Welcome to the Teacher's Recognition Day. As the spokesman of the Bureau of Education，I'd like to say "thank you" to Mrs. Zhang Guimei.

As is known，over the past months，Zhang's deeds _____ （report） widespread because of her selfless actions. The reason why her actions become a spotlight is that great contributions _____ （make） to girls' education by her over the years although she has gone through a rough patch. Actually，great emphasis _____ （not lay） on girls' education especially under-developed areas for many years. However，during the past twelve years，an example _____ （set） by Mrs. Zhang who shows us that it is not appropriate to place girls' education second to boys. Consequently，our inspiration and determination to emphasize girls' education_____ (stir) by her efforts since 3 years ago. More education-related facilities and financial support _____ (put) into use since last year. More importantly, social wider appeal to girls' education _____ (arouse) recently.

All in all, since holding the firm belief that education is the fairest shortcut to success regardless of boys or girls, Mrs Zhang's energy and enthusiasm _____ (devote) to her lifelong pursuit. She who went through the sacrifice and obstacles deserves the admiration and respect.

【Design intention】For the activity 1 and 2, by filling in the blanks cooperatively, students will be provided the related context to learn the structure and usage of the present perfect passive voice effectively. Meanwhile, students are offered a chance to consolidate what they've internalized and digested. Hence, students will be provided opportunities to learn how to use the structure effectively in an open atmosphere. At the same time they are encouraged to take an active part in the activities. For the activity 3, by filling in the blanks individually, students will digest the grammar by independent thinking.

Step 4. Pair work：Recite the speech again and do an interview.

(Student A and Student B take turns to act as the Reporter and the Spokesman.)

An interview:

The Reporter：Mr. Li, thanks for your speech. I'm a reporter from CCTV-1. May I ask you three questions?

The Spokesman：Sure.

The Reporter：So why do Mrs Zhang's deeds become a spotlight?

The Spokesman：...

The Reporter：Why does the native Bureau of Education emphasize girls' education?

The Spokesman：...

The Reporter：What has been done by the native Bureau of Education to emphasize girls' education?

The Spokesman：...

The Reporter: Thanks for your sharing.

Attention:

The student who acts as the Spokesman should use the present perfect passive voice.

【Design intention】By filling in the blanks in pairs, students will be provided the related context to check whether they really know the structure of the present perfect passive voice and then internalize the grammar themselves. By performing the interview, students are offered a chance to consolidate what they've internalized. At the same time they are inspired to think about their own inner thoughts, thus arousing their desire to share their ideas about what great deeds have been done by Mrs. Zhang.

Step 5. Writing.

If you were the right reporter, you would be asked to write a report about Mrs. Zhang's deeds to CCTV-1. Please compose the report.

Attention:

1. Please try to use the present perfect passive voice as much as possible.

2. Every correct present perfect passive voice is worth 10 points.

【Design intention】This part is designed to help students to put what they have learned into practical use. Meanwhile, students are expected to express themselves in English correctly by using the grammar, which is indispensable for them to form an English thinking mode and understand the difference between Chinese and English better.

Step 6. Presentation.

Two students are invited to share their reports and others try to give some comments.

Step 7. Homework.

Polish your report and read it to your friends.

第四节　现在进行时的被动语态

教学设计——新闻发布会

Step 1. Lead-in：Listen and fill in the blanks.

Good afternoon, everyone. Welcome to today's NPC&CPPCC press conference. As the host, I'm honored to shoulder the responsibility to host today's conference.The procedures will be launched as follows. To begin with, Minister of the Health Department declares what _____ （do） at present to promote nationwide hygiene. In addition, Minister of the Education Department claims what measures _____ （take） now to strive for an upward educational system. Afterwards, you'll be given a chance to share your opinions concerning conducive actions that _____ （put） currently. Simultaneously, if health and education-related questions _____ （ask） now, please wait after the two Ministers accomplish their speeches. Well, let's proceed with them step by step.

【Design intention】 The purpose of listening to the clip is to introduce the teaching target—the present progressive passive voice in this class. Students are expected to fill in the blanks with "be being done" introducing the present progressive passive voice.

Step 2. Read and fill，and then discuss and do an interview.

Activity 1. Read the speech and fill in the blanks in groups.

Good afternoon, everyone,

As Minister, I'm honored to make an announcement relevant to our nationwide hygiene about what _____ （do） at present. Primarily, a more completely medical system covering nationwide whether in urban or rural areas _____ （set up） currently. Additionally, vaccines related to basic antibodies _____ （study） by scientists. Ultimately, a whole nation citizens' healthy condition question-and-answer research_____ (survey) now. Most importantly, a more comprehensive welfare policy including residents' medical insurance_____ (discuss) now.

Thanks for your listening and attention. Questions related to my speech are warmly welcomed.

Activity 2. Do an interview.

Journalist A: Good afternoon, distinguished Minster. Just as you declaim to us, is it true that people in under-privileged areas can have access to a more complete medical system?

Minster: Absolutely, ...

Journalist B: Good afternoon, respected Minster. What kind of research is being surveyed now?

Minster: Well, ...

Journalist C: Good afternoon, Minster. Actually, I know some vaccines _____ (take) now to fight against COVID-19. Can you share us more about what _____ (do) to cope with this troublesome issue?

Minster: Yes, ...

Attention:

Please use the present progressive passive voice.

【Design intention】For the activity 1, by filling in the blanks cooperatively, students will be provided the related context to learn the structure and usage of the present progressive passive voice effectively. For the activity 2, students will be given a chance to put what they've learned into practical use. Hence, students will be provided opportunities to learn how to use the present progressive passive voice effectively in an open atmosphere. At the same time they are encouraged to take an active part in the activities.

Step 3. Practice: Read another speech and do an interview.

Activity 1. Fill in the blanks individually and do an interview in groups.

Good afternoon, everyone!

A saying _____ (quote) now to describe the current situation of Chinese education, that is, a promising education reform _____ (launch) by a powerful country. Undoubtedly, China's education mode _____ (introduce) by other countries at present. In order to become better, the following two measures_____ (take) by the Education Department.

For one thing, more financial policies related to teachers' welfare _____ (draft) at present. For another, the proposal concerning the equal access to education resources whether in rural or urban areas_____ (formulate) by the Education Department.

In a word, the whole Education Department staff's attention_____ (put) now to fulfil this goal.

Activity 2. Free talk (pair work).

If you were Minster of Education Department, would you please put forward more detailed measures to better education environment using one or two present progressive passive voice ?

Eg 1: students' overall development ——➤ put into practice

Students' overall development is being put into practice now.

Eg 2: after-school time in primany school ——➤ reduce in Shanghai

Eg 3: the reform of National Entrance Examination ——➤ carry out

Eg 4: the level of exams ——➤ upgrade

Eg 5: education-related facilities ——➤ improve

Eg 6: a more scientific academic evaluation system ——➤ set up

Attention:

Please use present progressive passive voice.

【Design intention】By filling in the blanks individually, students will be provided the related context to check if they really know the structure of the present progressive passive voice and then internalize the grammar themselves. By performing the pair work, students are offered a chance to consolidate what they've internalized. At the same time they are inspired to think about their own inner thoughts, thus arousing their desire to share their ideas about what is being done to better education.

Step **4**. Writing.

If you were a reporter from CCTV-9, you were expected to broadcast a report about what is being done by the Department of Health and the Department of Education now according to what you have listened on the spot.

Attention:

1. Please try to use present progress passive voice as much as possible.

2. Every correct present progressive passive voice is worth 10 points.

【Design intention】This part is designed to help students to put what they have learned into practical use. Meanwhile, students are expected to express themselves in English correctly by using the grammar, which is indispensable for them to form an English thinking mode and understand the difference between Chinese and English better.

Step **5**. Presentation.

Two students are invited to share their compositions and others try to make them better.

Step **6**. Homework.

Polish your report about what is being done by the Department of Health and the Department of Education.

第四章

非谓语动词教学设计

第一节　v-ing形式作主语和宾语

教学设计一——动物保护

Step 1. Lead-in：Show students a picture about WWF.

【Design intention】The picture is about WWF，which is an organization to protect the wildlife. Through looking at the picture，students can be led to the topic about this grammar learning class. Besides，it aims to stimulate students'enthusiasm in this class.

Step 2. Read the letter carefully and answer the questions.

Dear WWF，

Nowadays，many wild animals are endangered. Their habitats are threatened and the number of them is decreasing. Some people even kill them for their fur and meat. So I am writing to give you some suggestions about how to protect wildlife.

First，I suggest setting up natural reserves for them so that we can inspect them every month and see how fit they are. Second，making laws is an effective way to protect the wild animals. In that way，government can also use laws to punish those who hunt the wild animals illegally. Third，people should stop buying any product made of wild animals. If so, many wild animals can be better protected. Finally, the government should pay attention to raising people's awareness of protecting the wildlife. Because protecting wildlife is protecting ourselves.

I hope these suggestions will be helpful.

Yours,

Li Hua

Questions:

1. What is the letter mainly about? Are there any wild animals endangered in your hometown?

2. How many suggestions are mentioned in the letter? Please underline and read out.

【Design intention】 The purpose of reading the letter is to introduce the teaching target—v-ing form as subject and object in this class. Students are encouraged to find out the answers expressed with the v-ing form as subject and object.

Step 3. Complete the news according to the given words.

Tianjin: Protecting wildlife and forest resources and building environmentally-friendly city.

In recent years, Tianjin has made great efforts to protect its wildlife and forest resources, and is working on _____ (build oneself into) an environmentally-friendly city.

During the "13th Five-Year Plan" period, Tianjin pays attention to _____ (protect) ecology a lot. By _____ (carry out) strict protection measures and _____ (improve) its natural environment, wildlife has received effective protection. The number and diversity of wild birds have increased greatly.

In the future, _____ (promote) the protection of its wildlife resources will be continued in Tianjin by _____ (strengthen) wetland conservation, _____ (raise) public awareness, and _____ (make) relevant laws.

【Design intention】 In this part, students are expected to fill in the blanks according to the given words, which is the reappearance and reinforcement of the grammar and aims to help students understand the v-ing form as subject and object again by doing the exercise.

Step 4. Interview.

Imagine you are a reporter, and you want to interview a citizen in Tianjin to learn more about wildlife protection in his/her city. Be sure your interview includes as many v-ing forms as subject and object as possible.

Example：

Reporter：I heard that your city is taking action to protect the wildlife. What's your opinion on hunting?

Citizen：I think we should stop hunting wild animals.

Reporter：Why do you think so?

Citizen：Because I realize that protecting wildlife is protecting ourselves.

Reporter：OK, and what do you think we can do to prevent people from hunting wild animals?

Citizen：Er, for example, I suggest ...

【Design intention】In this interview, students are supposed to read the news with the v-ing form as subject and object to understand and feel the rules of the v-ing form as subject and object. And then, students are expected to complete the interview after their understanding.

Step 5. Discussion.

1. Discuss in groups to find the problems and suggestions about wildlife protection. (Each group is given one picture about wild animals that are harmed.)

2. One group finds a reporter to do an oral report to the class. Be sure the oral report includes as many v-ing forms as subject and object as possible.

Example：

Our group has learned that wild animals are being killed for their meat and fur. It is harmful to our environment and us human beings. Because protecting the wild animals is protecting ourselves. We have the following suggestions. First, we suggest stopping buying any product made of wild animals. Second, setting up more reserves is also good to protect wild animals. Third, ...

【Design intention】By making the oral report, students can get a better understanding step by step，which is helpful to build their confidence. Meanwhile，the discussion can let students express themselves freely，which can make students more interested and active to be involved in the class.

Step 6. Homework.

Make a poster about protecting the wildlife.

【Design intention】Homework is used to help students consolidate what they have learned and also help them develop their creative thinking.

教学设计二——体育明星

Step 1. Lead-in：A guessing game.

1. He was born in Shanghai and he loves playing basketball very much.

2. He started playing basketball when he was eight years old.

3. Since then，getting up early has become his habit.

4. When he grew up，playing basketball became his career.

5. He is famous for being the tallest basketball player in China.

【Design intention】The game is designed to be a lead-in of the target grammar. The five sentences contain two v-ing forms as the subject and three v-ing forms as the object，which can function as a basis of what is going to be taught in this class. Besides，the answer to the riddle，Yao Ming，is familiar to students, so that more students are willing to take an active part in the acitivty and at the same time it motivates students' interest in this class.

Step 2. Read the sentences again and pay attention to the underlined words.

1. Yao Ming loves playing basketball very much.

2. Yao Ming started playing basketball when he was eight years old.

3. Since then，getting up early has become one of his habits.

4. When Yao Ming grew up，playing basketball became his career.

5. Yao Ming is famous for being the tallest basketball player in China.

【Design intention】The main purpose of this step is to develop students' observing and summarizing ability. Through the underlined words of the five sentences, students can clearly draw the conclusion that the v-ing form can be used as the subject and should be treated as a singular. Also, it can be used as the object of prepositions and some transitive verbs.

Step 3. Read the material and fill in the blanks.

In 2002, Yao Ming finished _____ (study) his course and succeeded in _____ (join) the NBA. _____ (step) into NBA is not only a chance but also a challenge. _____ (fight) for the honor of China is always his goal. Devoted to _____ (realize) his dream, he was never absent from daily training. For basketball players, everyone can't avoid _____ (get) injured. However, he never considered _____ (give) it up. Nowadays, he has proved to everyone that _____ (be) tallest is not only in height but also in contribution. After _____ (retire) from the NBA, he enjoys _____ (work) as a coach to train more outstanding basketball players.

【Design intention】In this part, students are expected to fill in the blanks for the purpose of training their ability of knowledge transfer. On the basis of the second part, students can easily find that the v-ing forms are used to be filled in every blank. After the completion of the exercises, students can unconsciously know some transitive verbs followed by v-ing forms as the object.

Step 4. Interview.

Activity 1. Work in groups to participate in a role-play game where one student acts as a reporter Li Hua and the other one as Yao Ming. Then finish a dialogue.

L: How often do you play basketball?

Y: I insist on _____ (play) every day.

L: Have you ever intended to stop to have a rest?

Y: Actually, I have never considered _____ (give up).

L: What do you think is the real sports spirit?

Y: _____ is the real sports spirit for me. (try the best)

L: Do you play basketball with the purpose of winning fame?

Y：I enjoy _____（sweat）on the basketball court instead of

_____（win）fame.

L：What will make you excited when playing basketball?

Y：_____（defeat）opponents will make me feel excited.

L：What's your hope for Chinese basketball career?

Y：I'm looking forward to _____（see）a bright future.

Activity 2. Ask two pairs of students to share their dialogues.

【Design intention】By making the dialogue, students can apply what they have just learned to oral English and get a better understanding of the v-ing form as the subject and the object step by step, which is helpful for building their confidence and a sense of achievement. Meanwhile, it can contribute to forming an English thinking mode and improving their spoken English.

Step 5. Writing.

Supposing you are the interviewer Li Hua, after finishing the interview, try to complete the interview draft according to step 4, whose beginning and ending have been given.

Hello, everyone! I'm Li Hua, a journalist from China Daily. Today is March 26 and I just finished an exciting interview with Yao Ming, the most outstanding Chinese basketball player, in which he shared some stories between him and basketball. More details are as follows.

Yao Ming has insisted on playing basketball every day since he was 8 _____

_____

_____

_____

_____

_____

It is because of the efforts made by such outstanding athletes like Yao Ming that China's sports career can be a great success. We should also learn from their spirit and apply it to our field. That's all for the interview and thanks for your attention.

【Design intention】In this part, students are expected to complete the main body of an interview draft by making use of the dialogue in the step 4. The purpose of this writing is to offer the students another chance to help them consolidate what they have learned in this class and improve their writing skills. It can also arouse students' admiration and pride for the spirit of the great Chinese athletes.

Step 6. Sharing time.

Two students share their compositions and others make comments and help to polish their works in the class.

One possible version：

Hello everyone, I'm the journalist, Li Hua. Today is March 26 and I just finished an exciting interview with Yao Ming, the most outstanding Chinese basketball player, in which he shared some stories between him and basketball. More details are as follows.

Yao Ming has insisted on playing basketball every day since he was 8, which requires lasting patience and persistence. However, he has never considered giving up to have a rest. As far as Yao Ming is concerned, trying the best is the real sports spirit that every athlete should have. Instead of winning for fame, Yao Ming plays basketball because he enjoys sweating on the basketball court and defeating opponents will make him feel excited. As a pioneer of Chinese basketball, Yao Ming is looking forward to seeing more excellent basketball players and a bright future in Chinese sports field.

It is because of the efforts made by such outstanding athletes like Yao Ming that China's sports career can be a great success. We should also learn from their spirit and apply it to our field. That's all for the interview and thanks for your attention.

【Design intention】In this part, students will be improved by giving and accepting comments to make them have a better understanding of what they have learned in this class.

Step 7. Homework.

Polish your writing according to the comments given by your classmates and the teacher after class and hand it in to the teacher on schedule.

第二节 v-ing形式作表语、定语和宾语补足语

教学设计一——课堂学习

Step 1. Lead-in：Free talk.

Teacher：Boys and girls，what do you think of the English class?

Student 1：Ms. Liu，your English class is very interesting！I like your lesson！

Teacher：Oh，really? I'm very happy you like it.

Student 2：Sometimes it is boring，I think.

Teacher：Oh，I am sorry to hear that. Do you have any suggestions?

Student 3：If only you could play more interesting movies for us！

Teacher：I will consider that. To make my lessons more interesting，I will plan to offer you more learning materials appealing to high school students.

...

【Design intention】The free talk can get students involved in the topic of this class. Besides，it can make students experience the grammar.

Step 2. Discussion.

Imagine you are one of the students in the dialogue，and please give more suggestions to your English teacher and give your reasons at the same time.

1. Discuss in groups of 4 to give suggestions to your English teacher and show your reasons.

2. The reporter in the group shows the suggestions and reasons. Be sure to use as many v-ing forms as object complement，predicative and attribute as possible.

Example：

Our group thinks it is a good idea to play some interesting movies. Because we find interesting movies can make the class inviting. For example，my favorite actor is

145

Charlie Chaplin. His <u>charming</u> character is loved by many people and his subtle acting made everything <u>entertaining</u>. And I also think his movies are <u>amusing</u> and humorous.

【Design intention】This discussion can make students know how to use the grammar in real language context.

Step 3. Fill in the blanks according to the given words.

Suggestion 1: Pictures.

You'd better show some pictures which are _____ (charm) and _____ (inspire). The reason why I give this suggestion is as follows. Some _____ (interest) pictures set students _____ (think) actively and get students _____ (have) the desire to learn something new in class.

Suggestion 2: Games.

Why not prepare some games that are _____ (please) and _____ (encourage) in class? As far as I am concerned, some _____ (entertain) games have students _____ (take) part in class actively. Besides, some games make students cooperate with each other quite well in class.

Suggestion 3: Songs.

Why don't you play some _____ (charm) songs in class? It is believed that some beautiful songs are _____ (relax) and _____ (please), which can make students get involved in class quickly. What's more, some students who think English is difficult to learn may sometimes feel English class is _____ (tire). So these pleasing songs can let them relax in class.

【Design intention】In this part, students are expected to fill in the blanks by using v-ing form as object complement, predicative and attribute to consolidate the usage of this grammar.

Step 4. Interview.

Knowing Mary has put forward some practical suggestions to her English teacher, the reporter in the school newspaper wants to interview her. Now work in pairs to prepare for your interview. Make sure your dialogue includes as many v-ing forms as object complement, predicative and attribute as possible. You can begin your dialogue like this:

Reporter: Hi, Mary! I heard that you have put forward some practical suggestions to your English teacher. Can you share them with us?

Mary: Of course. First, I think it is a good idea to play some <u>interesting</u> movies. Because we find <u>amusing</u> movies can make the class <u>inviting</u>. For example, my favorite actor is Charlie Chaplin. His <u>charming</u> character is loved by many people and his subtle acting made everything <u>entertaining</u>. And I also think his movies are <u>entertaining</u> and humorous.

Reporter: Wow! That sounds really helpful.

Mary: Yes, I think so. And second...

Reporter: ...

【Design intention】The interview can help students consolidate the usage of the grammar in the real language context and can also practise their spoken English.

Step 5. Write your own suggestion letter to your English teacher.

Be sure to include as many v-ing forms as object complement, predicative and attribute as possible.

【Design intention】In this part, students are requested to write a suggestion letter, which can make students use this grammar in their writing. Thus, students can not only use the grammar in real language context, but also improve their writing ability.

Step 6. Homework.

Polish your writing after class.

【Design intention】Homework is used to help students consolidate what they have learned and also help them develop their writing ability.

教学设计二——新疆棉花

Step 1. Lead-in: Listen and fill in the blanks.

Good afternoon, everyone is welcomed to watch CCTV-9 whether on the spot or not. This is Economy Talks. We find many well-known stars _____（refuse） to cooperate with the famous brands such as Nike and Adidas today because a corporation named H&M issued a report. The report is_____ （amuse）, which claimed that the cottons produced in Xinjiang, China are _____ （exploit） cheap labor force. In order to seek the truth, our appointed journalist will interview one local Xinjiangnese and one manufacturer. First of all, let's look at the local_____ （spit） out the truth and the manufacturer_____ （share） his opinion with us. In addition, we'll be honored to listen to one distinguished economic critic_____ （comment） on this issue. Let's proceed with them step by step.

【Design intention】 The purpose of listening to the clip is to introduce the teaching target—the v-ing form as predicative and object complement in this class. Students are expected to fill in the blanks with v-ing form as predicative and object complement.

Step 2. Pair work: Work in pairs to ask and answer the following questions.

1. Why is the report amusing?

2. How will the appointed journalist seek the truth?

3. What will we be honored to listen to?

【Design intention】 By observing and answering the questions, students will have a basic understanding of the v-ing form as predicative and object complement. During this stage, students are encouraged to be familiar with the structure as well.

Step 3. Read and fill.

Activity 1. Read the dialogue and fill in the blanks and then do a role-play in groups.

The Journalist : Nice to meet you. I'm a journalist from CCTV-9. We can see now several foreign corporations _____ （refuse） to introduce cotton produced locally because they declare it's extremely labor-consuming. I'm wondering if you can show us the truth.

The Local: Sure. It is often the case that you can discover the advanced machines _____ （plant） cotton seeds at this moment. If you hear other manufacturers _____ （question） about it, please be sure to contact us.Why did the corporation H&M issue the false announcement? Today we hear the rumor _____ (spread) with evil purpose. We will keep ourselves _____ (illustrate) the truth to the public.

The Journalist: Thanks for your sharing. I do think so.

Activity 2. Read the other dialogue, and fill in the blanks and then do a role-play in groups.

The Journalist: Glad to see you. I'm a journalist from CCTV-9. We can see now several foreign corporations_____ (refuse) to introduce cotton produced in Xinjiang because they declare it's extremely labor-consuming. I'm wondering if you can share your opinion with us.

The Manufacturer: No problem. Now I observe many other countries _____ (plant) cotton seeds. Compared with others, China is undoubtedly _____ (adopt) a relatively effective and highly machined way. Meanwhile, today I hear the corporation H&M _____ (speak) ill words to abuse cotton produced in Xinjiang. Actually, as one of the manufacturers introducing cotton from Xinjiang, I have every reason to continue doing so because China is not what it used to be. Please be objective.

The Journalist: Thanks for your sharing. So it is.

Activity 3. Read a piece of speech and fill in the blanks individually.

Good afternoon, everyone. I'm Mr. Hong, a critic. From the two interviews, now we can notice the corporation H&M _____ (convey) false information to the world. If you are listening to me _____ (comment) on it now, you will discover more stars _____ (refuse) to continue the commercial contract. For one thing, our principle is _____ (offer) the high quality products without adopting the labor-consuming way. Simultaneously, we can see China _____ (develop) in a scientific and effective way nowadays, which seems to threaten other developed counties. Therefore, so-called anti-labor rights are _____ (spread). For another, many foreign countries are _____ (consider) China is an under-privileged country as they see many movies _____ (present) the under-developed scenes. Consequently, on the one hand, our primary job is _____ (develop) economy. On the other hand, whenever we catch others _____ (abuse) our country, we should take immediate measures to illustrate we are not what we used to be.

【Design intention】For the activity 1 and 2, by filling in the blanks cooperatively, students will be provided the related context to learn the structure and usage of the v-ing form as predicative and object complement effectively. Meanwhile, students are offered a chance to consolidate what they've internalized and digested. Hence, students will be provided opportunities to learn how to use the structure effectively in an open atmosphere. At the same time they are encouraged to take an active part in the activities. For the activity 3, by filling in the blanks individually, students will digest the grammar by independent thinking.

Step 4. Pair work：Read the speech again and do an interview.

(Student A and Student B take turns to act as the Journalist and the Critic.)

An interview：

The Journalist：Mr. Hong, thanks for your comments. After hearing you _____ (express) your ideas, may I ask you three questions?

The Critic：Sure.

The Journalist：So what's our principle?

The Critic：...

The Journalist：Why is so-called against labor rights announcement spreading?

The Critic：...

The Journalist：How can we illustrate we are not what we used to be?

The Critic：...

The Journalist：Thanks for your sharing.

【Design intention】By filling in the blanks in pairs, students will be provided the related context to check if they really know the structure of the v-ing form as predicative and object complement and then internalize the grammar themselves. By performing the interview, students are offered a chance to consolidate what they've internalized. At the same time they are inspired to think about their own inner thoughts, thus arousing their desire to know the basic reasons and the correct actions.

Step 5. Writing.

If you were the appointed journalist, you would be asked to write a report about the interviews and the comments to CCTV-9.

Attention：

1. Please try to use the v-ing forms as predicative and object complement as many as possible.

2. Every correct v-ing form as predicative and object complement is worth 10 points.

【Design intention】This part is designed to help students to put what they have learned into practical use. Meanwhile, students are expected to express themselves in English correctly by using the target grammar, which is indispensable for them to form an English thinking mode and understand the difference between Chinese and English better.

Step 6. Presentation.

Two students are invited to share their reports while others should listen carefully and try to give some comments.

Step 7. Homework.

Polish your report about the interviews and the comments to CCTV-9 and turn it in on time.

第三节　v-ing形式作状语

教学设计——网上购物

Step 1. Show students a video.

【Design intention】The video is about the advantages of online shopping, which can show students the topic about this grammar learning class. Besides, it aims to stimulate students' enthusiasm in this class.

Step 2. Ask students why so many people choose online shopping.

【Design intention】The question can enable students to talk about the advantages of online shopping by using adverbial clauses.

Step 3. Rewrite the adverbial clauses.

【Design intention】In this part, students are expected to rewrite the adverbial clauses by using v-ing form as adverbial.

Step 4. Show students a chart.

【Design intention】The chart is about people who are cheated when they buy things online, which can show students the disadvantages of online shopping.

Step 5. Ask students why so many people are cheated when they choose online shopping.

【Design intention】The question can enable students to talk about the disadvantages of online shopping by using adverbial clauses.

Step 6. Rewrite the adverbial clauses.

【Design intention】In this part, students are expected to rewrite the adverbial clauses by using v-ing form as adverbial.

Step 7. Fill in the blanks according to the given words.

Part 1. Advantages about online shopping.

Online shopping has many advantages. Initially, _____ (save) time, many people choose online shopping. _____ (buy) something, you just need to spend few minutes looking for your preference and click the buttons. Then you just need to stay at home _____ (wait) for its coming. Besides, you can compare the prices which are different in various shops _____ (find) the cheapest and the best ones. What's more, online shopping provides a way for those who live in remote places and have difficulty going shopping. Those people can choose and buy all kinds of goods they like _____ (click) the mouse gently.

Part 2. Disadvantages about online shopping.

Online shopping also has many disadvantages. Firstly, _____ (be) dishonest, they would not deliver the goods after paying. And if this situation happens, the consumers would be depressed and find nowhere to complain. Second, _____ (see) the goods rather than touching them, we may have false views and then make wrong decisions. Thirdly, most goods that are shown on the Internet are different from the true things, _____ (make) some customers unsatisfied when they receive the goods.

【Design intention】In this part, students are expected to fill in the blanks according to the given words, which are about the advantages and disadvantages of online shopping and aim to help students understand the v-ing form as adverbial again by doing the exercise.

Step **8**. Debate.

Discuss in groups to determine whether you support online shopping or not and then prepare for the debate.

Choose 4 representatives to take part in the debate.

Debater 1: Give a general idea about your group's idea.

Debater 2: Give some examples to support your group's idea.

Debater 3: Give some examples to support your group's idea.

Debater 4: Summarize your group's idea.

Attention:

Use v-ing forms as adverbial as many as possible when you do your debate.

You can begin your debate like this:

Debater 1: Hello, everyone! With the development of the Internet, more and more people tend to shop on the Internet. Online shopping has provided some benefits for us. Therefore, our group argue that...

Debater 2 & Debater 3: There are many examples where online shopping has provided some benefits in our daily life. For example, ...

Debater 4: As far as we are concerned, we should see the online shopping in an optimistic way. Providing so many benefits, online shopping has been popular in our daily life. Using it properly, it can benefit our daily life.

【Design intention】In this debate, students are expected to express their own views about online shopping by using v-ing form as adverbial, which can help students to use the target grammar in real language context.

Step 9. Homework.

Write a composition to show advantages, disadvantages ang your own opinion about online shopping. Be sure to use as many v-ing forms as adverbial as possible.

第四节　过去分词作定语和表语

教学设计一——嫦娥五号

Step 1. Lead-in：A guessing game.

1. It is an unmanned spacecraft.

2. It is the most technologically-advanced space project in China.

3. It is a mission（任务）launched to collect soil samples on the moon and to analyze the origin of the moon.

4. It is a space project named after the ancient Chinese goddess of the moon.

5. If this mission is successful，people all over the world will be excited and inspired.

6. The great scientists who made contributions to the space project are devoted and focused.

7. It will be a great scientific breakthrough remembered by generation after generation.

【Design intention】A guessing game is used to introduce the past participle as the attribute and predicative in this class and arouse students' interest as well.

Step 2. Read and summarize.

1. It is a spacecraft which is unmanned.

　　⟶ It is an unmanned spacecraft.

2. It is a space project which is the most technologically-advanced in China.

→ It is the most technologically-advanced space project in China.

3. It is a mission that/which is launched to collect soil samples on the earth and to analyze the origin of the moon.

→ It is a mission launched to collect soil samples on the moon and to analyze the origin of the moon.

4. It is a space project which is named after the ancient Chinese goddess of the moon.

→ It is a space project named after the ancient Chinese goddess of the moon.

5. It will be a great scientific breakthrough which is remembered by generation after generation.

→ It will be a great scientific breakthrough remembered by generation after generation.

6. If this mission is successful, people all over the world will be _____ (excite) and _____ (inspire).

→ If this mission is successful, people all over the world will be excited and inspired.

7. The great scientists who made contributions to the space project are _____ (devote) and _____ (focus).

→ The great scientists who made contributions to the space project are devoted and focused.

Summary:

1. It is an unmanned spacecraft. (past participle as prepositive attribute)

2. It is the most technologically-advanced space project in China. (past participle as prepositive attribute)

3. It is a mission launched to collect soil samples on the moon and to analyze the origin of the moon. (past participle as post-positive attribute)

4. It is a space project named after the ancient Chinese goddess of the moon. (past participle as post-positive attribute)

5. It will be a great scientific breakthrough remembered by generation after generation. (past participle as post-positive attribute)

155

6. If this mission is successful, people all over the world will be excited and inspired. (past participle as predicative)

7. The great scientists who made contributions to the space project are devoted and focused. (past participle as predicative)

【Design intention】In this part, students will have a basic understanding of the past participle as attribute and predicative through observation and discovery, and then they will have the ability to conclude basic rules of the past participle as attribute and predicative.

Step 3. Practice: Combine the sentences and use these sentences to deliver a speech.

Activity 1. Work in groups to combine the two sentences or fill in the blanks using the past participle as the attribute or predicative according to the given information in the envelop.

1. With the development of human society, there were a lot of scientific breakthroughs.

These breakthroughs were made by a group of great scientists.

2. It is because of those scientists that we can live a comfortable and convenient life now.

Those scientists are devoted and truly respected.

3. Those scientists are the pioneers and heroes.

They are remembered by everyone.

4. Nowadays, there are also a group of people.

They are inspired by the indomitable enterprising spirit.

5. With their efforts and cooperation, Chang'e 5 finally succeeded.

Chang'e 5 is designed to take soil samples from the moon.

6. They never give up even when they get _____ (frustrate) and feel _____ (depress).

7. On hearing the news, everyone was _____ (move) to tears.

Requirements:

1. The students who combine the two sentences or fill in the blanks must use the

past participle as the attribute or predicative.

2. The students who combine the two sentences or fill in the blanks explain why they combine them or fill in the blanks in this way.

Example：

1. In the development of human society, there were a lot of scientific breakthroughs made by a group of great scientists.

2. It is because of those devoted and truly respected scientists that we can live a comfortable and convenient life now.

3. Those scientists are the pioneers and heroes remembered by everyone.

Activity 2. Read the whole sentence in class and other students decide whether it is right.

Activity 3. Discuss with your group members about what you would say to introduce the great scientists and the space project in an award ceremony if you are given a chance to be a host.

Every group leader speaks out their introduction.

Example：

From the time when humans came into being to the time when we are living a comfortable life now, we human beings have experienced a lot of scientific breakthroughs, which make it possible for our society to develop...

【Design intention】By working with the group members, students will be provided with opportunities to learn the past participle as the attribute and predicative effectively in an open and happy atmosphere. At the same time they are encouraged to take an active part in the activities.

Step 4. Writing.

Supposing you are Dong Qin, host of the Spring Festival Gala, who is going to introduce Chang'e 5 and its team, please write down the short speech based on what we have talked about above.

Attention：

1. Please try to use the past participle as the attribute or predicative as much as possible.

2. Every correct past participle as the attribute or predicative is worth 10 points.

【Design intention】The purpose of this writing is to give the students another chance to help them consolidate what they have learned in this class and at the same time arouse their cultural sense and national pride, namely "using English to tell stories of our Chinese". Certainly, their creative thinking will be developed during their writing.

Step 5. Presentation.

Two students are invited to share their speeches and others try to help them make them better.

Step 6. Homework.

Polish your speech and try to introduce Chang'e 5 and its team clearly.

教学设计二——钟南山

Step 1. Lead-in：A guessing game.

Who is he?

1. He is a medical scientist loved and respected by all of us.

2. In the epidemic prevention and control, people were shocked by this 84-year-old man.

3. Most people were inspired and moved by his deeds.

【Design intention】A guessing game is used to introduce the teaching target in this class and cultivate the quality of students.

Step 2. Read, experience and analyze.

Read the short introduction about Zhong Nanshan.

Last year, I was <u>impressed</u> with the old man <u>called</u> Zhong Nanshan, a famous medical scientist in China. He is an old man <u>aged</u> 84 and graduated from Peking University in 1960. Meanwhile, he has been <u>devoted</u> to doing some research <u>related</u> to the respiratory illness（呼吸系统疾病）.

Task 1. Read the passage and pick out all the past participles.

Task 2. Experience the function of each past participle in the passage.

【Design intention】This part helps students understand the function of the past participle in the passage and experience the usage of it.

Step 3. Practice：Help students to know Zhong Nanshan deeply.

During the outbreak of the COVID-19，what did Zhong Nanshan do?

Task 3. Fill in the blanks and pay more attention to what you fill in.

After the outbreak of the COVID-19，Zhong Nanshan ignored his safety and headed for the area _____（expose）to the disease—Wuhan by himself. It was becauseof his deeds that thousands of _____（terrify）people were _____（inspire）. During the epidemic（疫情），he，along with his team，was _____（devote）to doing the research on finding the cure for the _____（terrify）disease. Meanwhile，the effective measures _____（put）forward by him helped the _____（affect）people. Undoubtedly，with the help of him and more medical workers，the number of _____（confirm）cases was once reduced.

The answers：exposed，terrified，inspired，devoted，terrifying，put，affected，confirmed

Task 4. Read the passage and answer the following questions with the past participle as attribute and predicative.

1. After the outbreak of the COVID-19，where did Zhong Nanshan go?

2. How did most of the people feel during the epidemic?

3. What did Zhong Nanshan and his team do during the outbreak of the COVID-19?

4. With the help of Zhong Nanshan and medical workers，who were cured? Why do you admire him?

Task 5. Group work.

Give students some words and ask them to use them to discuss the problem. Meanwhile，students need to use past participle as attribute and predicative.

inspire, move, respect, impress, expose, terrify, affect...

Eg. More and more people were inspired by his deeds and participated in the fight.

【Design intention】By doing some exercise and imitating the sentences, students will be provided opportunities to learn to use past participle as attribute and predicative effectively in the heuristic ways. At the same time they are encouraged to take an active part in the activities.

Step 4. Writing.

In the fight of the COVID-19, we all know the hero—Zhong Nanshan. Please write a short passage about him.

Requirements：

1. Give a brief introduction.

2. What did he do during the outbreak of the infectious disease?

3. Why did he become a national hero?

Attention：

1. Please try to use the past participle as attribute and predicative as much as possible.

2. Every correct sentence using the target grammar is worth 10 points.

【Design intention】The purpose of this writing is to give the students another chance to help them consolidate the past participle as attribute and predicative in this class and at the same same arouse their national pride, and stimulate them to follow Zhong Nanshan's example to make contributions to our motherland in the future.

Step 5. Presentation.

Two students share their writings and others try to help them make the writing better.

Step 6. Homework.

Polish your writing and also you can ask your teacher to give you some help.

第五节　过去分词作宾语补足语

教学设计一——特色小吃

Step 1. Lead-in：A guessing game.

What is it for breakfast?

Clues：

1. People have it made from flour or rice.

2. You see this snack served cold or hot.

3. You find this snack eaten as breakfast everywhere in Ankang.

It is steamed noodles.

【Design intention】The answer to this guessing game is steamed noodles, which are a kind of local snack. This topic can surely stimulate the students' interest in this lesson and encourage them to explore this topic.

Step 2. Read and answer questions.

Part 1.

The owner of the restaurant asked us to get in. She said she had to get all the preparations done before 6：30. First of all, she had the tables and chairs cleaned while her husband was getting the floor swept. She then went to the kitchen to have the paste steamed on the stove, after which, she had all the sauces well mixed. She took a deep breath when she found all the preparations finished.

1. What did the owner have to do before 6：30?

2. What did she do to the tables and chairs?

3. What did her husband do to the floor?

4. After cleaning, which two things did she do in the kitchen?

5. When did she take a deep breath?

Part 2.

It was 6: 30 and we finally got ourselves seated and began to eat. While enjoying our meals, we saw many other customers served by the owner. We also heard some of them told to wait when she was too busy. However, we noticed each customer welcomed by her warmly, so none of them was angry or impatient.

1. Who served the customers?

2. What did we hear when the owner was too busy?

3. Why wasn't each customer angry or impatient while waiting for their noodles?

【Design intention】The purpose of reading is to introduce the teaching target—past participle used as object complement in this class. Students are encouraged to find out the answers expressed with past participle used as object complement of the questions about the preparations the restaurant owner did and how she did her business.

Step 3. Complete the passage with the correct form of the verbs.

I am Miss Li and I run a steamed noodles restaurant close to Gao Xin Middle School. Every morning I get up around 5: 30 because I have to get all the preparations _____ (finish) before 6: 30. After arriving at my restaurant at 6: 00, I start my day. Firstly, I need to have all the tables and chairs _____ (clean) while my husband is getting the floor _____ (sweep). After that, I go to the kitchen to get the paste _____ (steam) on the stove. When I find all the preparations _____ (do), I can take a deep breath.

My customers come to eat around 6: 30 and when I see the first customer _____ (welcome) by my husband, I begin to get the noodles _____ (slice) and _____ (mix) with all the sauces. My husband is happy when he sees each customer _____ (serve) with their noodles. Sometimes he notices some of them _____ (tell) to wait when I am too busy. However, they are never angry or impatient because we always have them well _____ (serve).

【Design intention】In this part, students are expected to rewrite the passage imagining they were the restaurant owner. The reappearance and reinforcement of the grammar point aim to help students understand the past participle as object complement again by using the correct form of the verbs.

Step 4. Write a passage about how to make steamed noodles.

Look at the pictures of the process of making steamed noodles and write down the cooking instructions for each step.

1. Get the flour mixed with water and a little salt.

2. Have the paste spread evenly on the steaming plate.

3. Get the stove heated.

4. Have the pasted steamed for 15 minutes.

5. Get the pancake sliced into noodles.

6. Get the noodles well mixed with all the sauces.

【Design intention】In this step，students are supposed to write down sentences using past participle as object complement to put this grammar point into use. Writing in this way helps them to understand the target grammar and more importantly，enables them to get the hang of it.

Step 5. Homework.

Combine the sentences you just wrote to create a brief introduction to making steamed noodles. You should use past participle as object complement and add conjunctive words to make your passage smooth.

【Design intention】Homework helps the students to summarize what they have learnt and enables them to use the target grammar in real situations.

教学设计二——新疆棉花

Step 1. Lead-in：An introduction to a piece of news.

China is one of the world's major cotton producing countries with the total production accounting for one fourth of the world cotton production. And Xinjiang is China's largest cotton base，which gets its economy developed by providing high-quality cotton. However, several days ago, we <u>found our Xinjiang cotton boycotted</u> by some clothes brands such as H&M, Nike, etc., which claimed that there are forced labors in Xinjiang cotton production.

Amid the attacks from western countries on human rights, the Xinjiang Uygur autonomous regional government held talks in Urumqi on Friday <u>with more than 30 foreign diplomats invited</u> to visit the factories. Xinjiang is doing a good job and we believe before long we will <u>see greater achievements made</u> in its social and economic development.

For us Chinese people, we are sure to meet with a lot of challenges in realizing our Chinese Dream. What we need to do is to <u>make ourselves united</u> so that we can <u>make ourselves undefeated.</u>

【Design intention】This part is designed not only to help students know more about what is happening around the world, but also to introduce the focus of this class with a piece of news to arouse students' interest in grammar point: the past participle used as the object complement.

Step 2. Read and summarize.

1. And Xinjiang is China's largest cotton base, which <u>gets its economy developed</u> by providing high-quality cotton.

2. Several days ago, we <u>found our Xinjiang cotton boycotted</u> by some clothes brands such as H&M, Nike, etc.

3. The Xinjiang Uygur autonomous regional government held talks in Urumqi on Friday <u>with more than 30 foreign diplomats invited</u> to visit the factories.

4. Xinjiang is doing a good job and we believe before long we will <u>see greater achievements made</u> in its social and economic development.

5. What we need to do is to <u>make ourselves united</u> so that we can <u>make ourselves undefeated.</u>

Summary:

1. And Xinjiang is China's largest cotton base, which <u>gets its economy developed</u> by providing high-quality cotton.

(Its economy is developed.)

2. Several days ago, we <u>found our Xinjiang cotton boycotted</u> by some clothes brands such as H&M, Nike, etc.

(We found that our Xinjiang cotton is boycotted.)

3. The Xinjiang Uygur autonomous regional government held talks in Urumqi on Friday <u>with more than 30 foreign diplomats invited</u> to visit the factories.

(More than 30 foreign diplomats were invited.)

4. Xinjiang is doing a good job and we believe before long we will <u>see greater achievements made</u> in its social and economic development.

(Greater achievements will be made.)

5. What we need to do is to <u>make ourselves united</u> so that we can <u>make ourselves undefeated</u>.

(We are united; We are undefeated.)

【Design intention】 In this part, students will have a basic understanding of the past participle used as the object complement and then they will have the ability to conclude basic rules of the past participle used as the object complement.

Step 3. Practice: Combine the sentences and use these sentences to deliver a speech.

Activity 1. Work in groups to combine the information and make sentences using the past participle as the object complement according to the given information in the envelop.

1. China is a fast-developing country.

Countless and various natural resources are distributed nationwide.

2. If you travel around this nation, you will find...

You are attracted by various spectacular scenery and sights in different regions.

3. China is a big country.

The southeastern and coastal areas are populated by people.

4. You will find...

This country is made up of several provinces, including Taiwan.

5. Taiwan gets itself...

Taiwan is connected with other provinces and has been an indispensable part of China from ancient times.

6. The year 2021 has witnessed...

Poverty is eliminated.

7. China will soon make...

Chinese Dream will be realized.

Activity 2. Discuss with your group members about what you would say to introduce China to the world if you are given a chance to deliver a speech to them.

Requirements：

1. The students who make the sentences are expected to use the past participle as the object complement.

2. The students who combine the sentences need to explain why they combine them in this way.

Example：

China is a fast-developing country with countless and various natural resources distributed nationwide. If you travel around this nation, you will find yourself attracted by various spectacular scenery and sights in different regions. Having a large population, China is a big country with southeastern and coastal areas populated by people. If you look at the map, you will find this country made up of several provinces, including Taiwan. Historically, Taiwan gets itself connected with other provinces and has been an indispensable part of China from ancient times.

In recent years, China's economy, military force and technology are developing very fast, some of which have reached the world-leading level. Meanwhile, the year 2021 has witnessed poverty eliminated and this socialist society has got full development, which means that all Chinese people have totally got rid of hunger and poverty. We Chinese people have the confidence that China will soon make its Chinese Dream realized.

【Design intention】By working with the group members, students will be provided with opportunities to learn the past participle used as the object complement effectively in an open and happy atmosphere. At the same time they are encouraged to take an active part in the activities. "Practice makes perfect." Therefore, through practice, students can better understand how to use the past participle as the object complement.

Step **4**. Writing.

Nowadays，China is becoming more powerful and is playing an increasingly important role in international affairs，leading to Chinese status increasing rapidly. However，some western media and press distorted the facts and smeared China spitefully. Supposing you have a chance to introduce China to the world，what would you say to win China's image back?

Attention：

1. Please try to use the past participle as the object complement as much as possible.

2. Every correct past participle as the object complement is worth 10 points.

【Design intention】The purpose of this writing is to give the students another chance to help them consolidate what they have learned in this class and at the same time arouse their cultural awareness and national pride. Meanwhile，their creative thinking will be developed during their writing.

Step **5**. Presentation.

Two students share their speeches and others try to help them make it better.

Step **6**. Homework.

Polish your speech to win China's image back and speak it out in the class.

第六节　过去分词作状语

教学设计一——新冠病毒

Step **1**. Lead-in：Look at the pictures and answer the questions.

1. Why did we have online classes at the beginning of the year 2020?

（Because we were）Hit by the COVID-19，we had to stay at home for online classes.

2. Who made contributions to saving people in Wuhan? Did they feel frightened at that time?

The doctors and the nurses. (Although they were) Frightened by the deadly infectious disease, the doctors and nurses still chose to come to save the people infected by the COVID-19 in Wuhan.

3. Do you agree we were safer when we were compared with the nurses and doctors at that time?

Can't agree more. (When we were) Compared with the doctors and nurses in Wuhan at the beginning of the year 2020, we were much safer.

4. Do you think that we will defeat the COVID-19? When will we defeat the disease?

As far as I am concerned, (if we are) given more time, we human beings can finally defeat the COVID-19 in the end in the future.

【Design intention】 These questions are used to introduce the teaching target in this class and arouse students' interest as well.

Step 2. Read and summarize.

1. Because we were hit by the COVID-19, we had to stay at home for online classes.

Hit by the Covid-19, we had to stay at home for online classes.

2. Although they were frightened by the deadly infectious disease, the doctors and nurses still chose to come to save the people infected by the COVID-19 in Wuhan.

Frightened by the deadly infectious disease, the doctors and nurses still chose to come to save the people infected by the COVID-19 in Wuhan.

3. When we were compared with the doctors and nurses in Wuhan at the beginning of the year 2020, we were much safer.

Compared with the doctors and nurses in Wuhan at the beginning of the year 2020, we were much safer.

4. If we are given more time, we human beings can finally defeat the COVID-19

in the end in the future.

Given more time, we human beings can finally defeat the COVID-19 in the end in the future.

Summary:

(Because we were) Hit by the Covid-19, we had to stay at home for online classes.

(Although they were) Frightened by the deadly infectious disease, the doctors and nurses still chose to come to save the people infected by the COVID-19 in Wuhan.

(When we were) Compared with the doctors and nurses in Wuhan at the beginning of the year 2020, we were much safer.

(If we are) Given more time, we human beings can finally defeat the COVID-19 in the end in the future.

【Design intention】In this part, students will have a basic understanding of the past participle as the adverbial through observation and discovery, and then they will have the ability to conclude basic rules of the past participle as the adverbial.

Step 3. Practice: Combine the sentences and use these sentences to deliver a speech.

Activity 1. Work in groups to combine the two sentences using the past participle as the adverbial according to the given information in the envelop.

1. We were hit by the COVID-19.

We had to stay at home for online classes.

2. The doctors and nurses were frightened by the deadly infectious disease.

The doctors and nurses still chose to come to save the people infected by the COVID-19 in Wuhan.

3. We were compared with the doctors and nurses in Wuhan.

We were much safer at that time.

4. We are given more time.

We human beings can finally defeat the COVID-19 in the end in the future.

5. Many doctors and nurses were exhausted by long-term hard work.

Many doctors and nurses even fell fast asleep in the offices.

6. Many doctors' and nurses' faces were covered by the protective goggles.

Many doctors' and nurses' faces were left with deep masks, which is still very impressive.

7. Some westerners are warned of the COVID-19.

They still don't wear masks.

8. We are given a chance to say a few words to the doctors and nurses.

We would express thanks to them for what they have done for us.

Requirements:

1. The students who combine the two sentences must use the past participle as the adverbial.

2. The students who combine the two sentences need to explain why they combine them in this way.

Example:

Hit by the COVID-19, we had to stay at home for online classes.

Frightened by the deadly infectious disease, the doctors and nurses still chose to come to save the people infected by the COVID-19 in Wuhan.

Activity 2. Discuss with your group members about what you would say to the doctors and nurses if you are given a chance to deliver a speech to them.

Every group leader speaks out their gratitude to the doctors and nurses by using the past participle as much as possible after discussing with their group members.

Example:

We are grateful to all of you for what you have done for us. Frightened by the deadly infectious disease, the doctors and nurses still chose to come to save the people infected by the COVID-19 in Wuhan. Covered by the protective goggles, your faces were left with deep imprints. Exhausted by long-term hard work, you even fell fast asleep in the offices.

【Design intention】 By working with the group members, students will be provided opportunities to learn the past participle as the adverbial effectively in an open atmosphere. At the same time they are encouraged to take an active part in the activities. "Practice makes perfect." Therefore, through practice, students can better understand how to use the past participle as the adverbial.

Step 4. Writing.

Suppose you have got a chance to give a speech to the doctors and nurses in a meeting. And you need to express your thanks to the doctors and nurses and why you are grateful to them. Please write down the speech based on what we have talked about above.

Attention:

1. Please try to use the past participle as the adverbial as much as possible.

2. Every correct past participle as the adverbial is worth 10 points.

【Design intention】The purpose of this writing is to give the students another chance to help them consolidate what they have learned in this class and at the same time arouse their cultural awareness and national pride, namely "using English to tell stories of our Chinese". Of course, their creative thinking will be developed during their writing.

Step 5. Presentation.

Two or three students share their speech and others try to help them make corrections.

Step 6. Homework.

Write a letter to express your thanks to the doctors and nurses and explain the reasons.

教学设计二——未来生活

Step 1. Lead-in: Show some pictures chosen from movies and ask questions.

Have you ever watched the movie *Doraemon* and *Baymax*?

I really want a robot like Doraemon or Baymax because when exhausted after a day's work，I really need someone to comfort me and give me warmth. And I believe accompanied by my friend Baymax，I will feel at ease.

1. If you can have your own robot，what kind of robot would you like?

<u>Given the chance</u> to own a robot，I would like to have one that can wake me up in the morning and help me wash up when I still feel sleepy.

<u>Worried about my coming final exam</u>，I would like to create a robot which helps me learn all subjects.

<u>When asked to finish</u> an assignment that is hard to do，I wish I could be helped by a robot just like Doraemon which can do anything that seems impossible.

<u>Developed by an international company</u>，my robot will be good at cooking so that my mom can be freed from dull daily routine.

2. What will you do if you find yourself left alone on a deserted island?

<u>Left alone on a deserted island</u>，I won't lose hope and I'll practice useful life skills so that I can escape one day.

...

【Design intention】These questions are used to introduce the teaching target in this class and arouse students' interest as well.

Step 2. Read and summarize.

Given the chance to own a robot，I would like to have one that can wake me up in the morning and help me to wash up when I still feel sleepy.

Worried about my coming final exam，I would like to create a robot which helps me learn all subjects.

When asked to finish an assignment that is hard to do，I wish I could be helped by a robot just like Doraemon which can do anything that seems impossible.

Developed by an international company，my robot will be good at cooking so that my mom can be freed from dull daily routine.

Left alone on a deserted island，I won't lose hope and I'll practice useful life skills so that I could escape one day.

Summary：

（If I am）Given the chance to own a robot，I would like to have one that can wake me up in the morning and help me to wash up when I still feel sleepy.

（Because I am）Worried about my coming final exam, I would like to create a robot which helps me learn all subjects.

（When I am）Asked to finish an assignment that is hard to do, I wish I could be helped by a robot just like Doraemon which can do anything that seems impossible.

（My robot will be）Developed by an international company, my robot will be good at cooking so that my mom can be freed from dull daily routine.

（Although I am）Left alone on a deserted island, I won't lose hope and I'll practice useful life skills so that I can escape one day.

【Design intention】In this part, students will have a basic understanding of the past participle as the adverbial through observation and discovery, and then they will have the ability to conclude basic rules of the past participle as the adverbial.

Step 3. Practice: Combine the sentences and use these sentences to deliver a speech.

Activity 1. Work in groups to combine the two sentences using the past participle as the adverbial according to the given information in the envelop.

1. Life is advanced by technology.

Life in the future will be totally different from that at present.

2. We will be influenced by the prosperous economy.

All of us will be able to live more comfortably and happily.

3. The time machine is developed by an international company.

Time machine enjoys great popularity.

4. Education is supervised by the society and the government.

Education focuses on the happiness and healthy growth of teenagers instead of grades they get in the exams.

5. A special gate is specially designed to meet people's needs for traveling.

The special gate can take people to wherever they want to travel.

6. Many planets are explored by human beings.

These planets in the universe are developed into tourist attractions.

7. The problem is caused by the development of technology.

The problem of overusing natural resources and environmental pollution is becoming increasingly severe.

8. The technological weapon is left in the hands of terrorists.

The technological weapon can be so powerful as to destroy the world.

Requirements：

1. The students who combine the two sentences are expected to use the past participle as the adverbial.

2. The students who combine the two sentences need to explain why they combine them in this way.

Example：

Advanced by technology, life in the future will be totally different from that at present.

Influenced by the prosperous economy, all of us will be able to live more comfortably and happily.

Activity 2. Discuss with your group members about what you would say to the people if you should come from the future.

Example：

I am an ordinary student from the year of 2050 and it is my time machine that takes me here. Therefore, I'd like to share the life in the future with you so that you can develop the world better and avoid some possible risks that may ruin the world in the future.

...

【Design intention】By working with the group members, students will be provided opportunities to learn the past participle as the adverbial effectively in an open and happy atmosphere. At the same time they are encouraged to take an active part in the activities. "Practice makes perfect." Therefore, through practice, students can better understand how to use the past participle as the adverbial.

Step 4. Writing.

Suppose you are an ordinary student from the year of 2050 and it is the time machine that takes you to the year of 2021. Make a speech to the people living in this day and age, sharing the life in the future so that people can develop the world better and avoid some possible risks that may ruin the world in the future.

Attention:

1. Please try to use the past participle as the adverbial as much as possible.

2. Every correct past participle as the adverbial is worth 10 points.

【Design intention】The purpose of this writing is to give the students another chance to help them consolidate what they have learned in this class and at the same time arouse their cultural awareness, and their creative thinking will be developed during their writing.

Step 5. Presentation.

Two students share their speeches and others try to help them make it better.

Step 6. Homework.

Polish your speech and share it with your deskmate.

教学设计三——网上购物

Step 1. Read the passage and answer questions.

Sabrina is a lady addicted to online shopping. Attracted by the beautiful clothes, she has almost all her money spent in shopping. Sometimes, complimented by some sale women, she could buy many unnecessary goods and then throw them away, which causes waste. Worried about her safety and finance, her husband asks us to help her.

Questions:

1. What's Sabrina like?

⟶ Sabrina is a lady addicted to online shopping.

2. Why does she spend all her money in shopping?

⟶ Attracted by the beautiful clothes, she has almost all her money spent in shopping.

3. Why does she always buy wrong goods?

⟶ Complimented by some sale women, she could buy many wrong goods.

4. Why does her husband ask us to help her?

⟶ Worried about her safety and finance, her husband asks us to help her.

【Design intention】A short passage about Sabrina's excessive shopping is used to introduce the teaching target of this class and arouse students' interest as well.

Step 2. Observation and summarize.

1. Sabrina is a lady addicted to online shopping. (the past participle as the attribute)

2. Attracted by the beautiful clothes, she has almost all her money spent in shopping. (the past participle as the adverbial)

3. Complimented by some sale women, she could buy many wrong goods. (the past participle as the adverbial)

4. Worried about her safety and finance, her husband asks us to help her. (the past participle as the adverbial)

【Design intention】Through observation and discovery, students will have a basic understanding of the past participle as attribute and adverbial and then they will have the ability to conclude basic rules of the past participle as attribute and adverbial.

Step 3. Practice.

Activity 1. Fill in the following blanks with proper form of the given words.

1. The lady _____ (dress) in red is Sabrina.

2. Money _____ (earn) by her husband was all used to buy clothes by her.

3. She thinks the goods _____ (buy) online is cheaper and more fashionable.

4. _____ (face) with this problem, Sabrina's husband asks us to help her.

【Design intention】This short passage is used to test whether students have mastered the rules of the past participle as attribute and adverbial and also give some hints for the following activity.

Activity 2. Discuss with group of 6 to make a list of the advantages and disadvantages of online shopping.

Advantages	Disadvantages
Save time	Release personal information
Provide us with a wide range of products	Buy unnecessary things
Offer reasonable prices	Be cheated
Be convenient	Waste money

【Design intention】This activity can train students' oral expression and thinking ability by discussing the advantages and disadvantages of online shopping as well as offer some related materials for the following activity.

Activity 3. Based on the above discussion, choose proper verbs from the box to complete the sentences by using the past participle or present participle with group of 6.

order	provide	save	release	cheat
worry	give	look for	buy	

1. Once _____, it can be delivered directly to our home.

2. _____ a little time, we can search hundreds of shops online quickly.

3. _____ with a lot of goods, shoppers can find products meeting their needs.

4. It is convenient, and we can stay at home, _____ what we want to buy.

5. _____ time, shoppers can spend spare time in developing interest.

6. _____ too many goods, shoppers waste a lot of money.

7. Shoppers _____ online will suffer losses and find it hard to complain.

8. Person information _____ by sellers will leave shoppers in a dangerous situation.

9. _____ about the quality, more and more people are cautious about online shopping.

【Design intention】This activity can train students' language practice and organization ability by finishing sentences about the advantages and disadvantages of online shopping, and also these finished sentences can effectively lower the writing difficulty.

Step 4. Writing.

Write a letter to Sabrina, persuading her to consume rationally.

Requirement:

Please try to use the past participle as the attribute or adverbial as much as possible.

Dear Sabrina,

    Sorry to hear that you are addicted to online shopping. It is normal that, with the popularity of online shopping, many of us prefer to shop online. However, each coin has two sides.

    On the one hand, _____

_____

_____

    On the other hand, _____

_____

_____

    Hoping you can think it over before buying something online after reading this letter.

Yours,
Li Hua

【Design intention】This step is to give the students another chance to help them consolidate what they have learned in this class and at the same time train students' ability to use English to solve problems by persuading.

Step 5. Presentation.

Find some students to share their writing and others help them polish it.

Step 6. Homework.

Share your story with your partner to check whether there are some mistakes.

第五章

情态动词教学设计

第一节 may / might，can / could，will/ would，shall / should，must / can't

教学设计——端午节

Step 1. Lead-in：A guessing game.

Teacher's description：

1. It is a Chinese festival.

2. We will eat special food that day.

3. It is celebrated to honor a Chinese poet.

Students are requested to use the given sentence patterns to guess what it is：

1. It may/might/could/can't be...

2. Can/Could it be...?

3. It must/can't be...

【Design intention】A guessing game is used to activate the classroom atmosphere and introduce the teaching target of this class and arouse students' interest as well.

Step 2. Presentation.

Read the following sentences and choose the proper meaning to complete the following chart.

Group 1. can and could

1. He can speak English very well.

2. The teacher said that we could not leave early.

3. The hunters have been lost for days. They could starve.

4. Could you please show me the way?

Group 2. may and might

1. May I borrow the book?

2. I failed this time, but I might do better next time.

Group 3. will and would

1. My grandma will come for dinner.

2. Last year, he would get up at 7 every day.

3. Would you like to join our club?

Group 4. shall and should

1. We shall be there by 3 p.m.

2. You should arrive at the airport at least one hour early.

3. The teacher should be here soon.

Group 5. must and can't

1. You must be careful when crossing the street.

2. Li Hua has won the game three times. He must be very smart.

3. You must be joking. That can't be true.

Meanings：

A. Possibility	B. Ability	C. Advice	D. Guessing	E. Past habit
F. Necessity	G. Permission	H. Prediction	I. Promise	J. Request

Group member	Modal verbs	Meaning	
Group 1	can, could	1._____ 2._____	
		3._____ 4._____	

Group member	Modal verbs	Meaning		
Group 2	may, might	1. _____ 2. _____		
Group 3	will, would	1. _____ 2. _____ 3. _____		
Group 4	shall, should	1. _____ 2. _____ 3. _____		
Group 5	must, can't	1. _____ 2. _____ 3. _____		

【Design intention】In this part, students will have a basic understanding of the function and usage of the modal verbs（may/might, can/could, will/would, shall/should, must/can't）by analyzing the sample sentences.

Step 3. Practice.

Teacher：My American friend Henry is very interested in the Dragon Boat Festival, so we have a talk.

1. Use modal verbs to complete the dialogue. Some may have more than one answer.

Henry：Hey, Vanya. _____ I ask you something about the Dragon Boat Festival?

Vanya：Sure.

Henry：When will it be celebrated?

Vanya：It _____ be celebrated on the fifth day of the fifth lunar month.

Henry：_____ you please tell me the origin?

Vanya：Actually, we celebrate it in memory of a great poet, Qu Yuan.

Henry：OK, I see. What should you do that day?

Vanya：We will eat Zongzi and watch dragon boat races. Our family member _____ have a meal together and visit our relatives and friends.

Henry：That _____ be very interesting!

Vanya：So _____ you like to come and spend the festival with us?

Henry：Wow. I am really glad to hear that.

Vanya：Of course. I believe my family _____ be very surprised if you _____ come, and you _____ know more about Chinese cultures and enjoy yourself here.

Henry: I _____ wait to see you in China!

2. Students work in pairs to make the dialogue and check the answers with each other.

3. The teacher invites some students to present the dialogue as well as check the answers with the whole class.

【Design intention】This is a controlled exercise in which students will be provided with opportunities to use modal verbs in real-life conversations and by completing the dialogue, they will be aware of the similarities and differences between the modal verbs and use them correctly.

Step 4. Writing.

1. Write an email to introduce the festival and invite Henry to China. Use as many modal verbs as possible.

Linking words: First of all, besides, what's more, moreover, in addition, most importantly...

Dear Henry,

I am very glad to hear that you are interested in the Dragon Boat Festival, so I am writing this email to tell you something about it.

_____

_____

_____

_____

_____

_____

_____

Looking forward to your early reply.

Sincerely Yours,

_____

2. After writing, some students will be invited to share their compositions and the teacher and the other students will make some comments.

【Design intention】Through this less-controlled activity, students will be able to integrate what they've learned in previous activities to write an email of invitation so that they will have their comprehensive competences developed.

Step 5. Self-assessment.

In this lesson,

1. I have mastered the meaning and usage of modal verbs（may/might, can/could, will/would, shall/should, must/can't）. Yes./No.

2. I am able to talk about the Dragon Boat Festival using modal verbs. Yes./No.

3. I can write the email of invitation with modal verbs. Yes./No.

4. I think I could do better if I...

【Design intention】In this part, students will reflect on what they've learned in this class and know how to make improvements in future learning.

Step 6. Homework.

Individual task：Polish your writing and share it with your classmates.

Group task：Choose one of the situations（in the teachers' office, in the classroom, at home, at a store...）and create a dialogue. Try to use as many modal verbs as possible. You will present your dialogues in the next class.

【Design intention】Homework is used to help students consolidate what they have learned and also apply it to real-life situations.

第二节　ought to / ought not to，have to / don't have to，mustn't / needn't

教学设计一——健康生活

Step 1. Lead-in：Free talk.

Teacher：Must I lose weight?

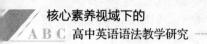

Students are requested to give their answers using some modal verbs.

【Design intention】A question about the teacher is used to activate the classroom atmosphere and introduce the teaching target of this class and arouse students' interest as well.

Step 2. Presentation.

Teacher：My mother always thinks I ought to lose wight. Yesterday she sent me a message like this.

I know you have to work hard，but you don't have to sit in your office all day. In other words，you needn't spend too much time sitting and you ought to spare some time for exercise. I want you to lose weight，but you mustn't be on a diet，which is not healthy.

Students are requested to complete the chart by reading and analyzing the message.

Modal verbs	Meaning
have to	
don't have to/needn't	
ought to/ought not to	
mustn't	

【Design intention】By observing and analyzing the sentences，students will have a basic understanding of the function and usage of the modal verbs（ought to，ought not to，have to，don't have to，mustn't and needn't）.

Step 3. Practice.

Teacher：My American friend Sam also had a talk with me on how to keep healthy.

1. Use modal verbs above to complete the dialogue. Some may have more than one answer.

Sam：Hello，teacher. I am too fat now and I know it's unhealthy. But what should I do?

Teacher：Well，you worry too much about it.

Sam： Could I try some medicine?

Teacher： No， you _____ do that， which will harm your body. You _____ have a balanced diet， which consists of energy-giving food， protective food and body-building food.

Sam： OK， what else should I do?

Teacher： You should do some exercise regularly although you _____ go on business often.

Sam： It's not easy for me. Shall we work out together?

Teacher： Sure. And most importantly， you _____ drink or smoke any more， for you must keep a good living habit.

2. Students work in pairs to make the dialogue and check the answers with each other.

3. The teacher invites some students to present the dialogue as well as check the answers with the whole class.

【Design intention】 This is a controlled exercise in which students will be provided with opportunities to use modal verbs in real-life conversations and by completing the dialogue， they will be aware of the similarities and differences between the modal verbs and use them correctly.

Step 4. Writing.

1. Write an email to Sam to give him some advice on keeping healthy. Use as many modal verbs as possible.

Some modal verbs we have learned： may/might， can/could， will/would， shall/ should， must/can't， ought to/ought not to， have to/don't have to， mustn't/ needn't...

Linking words： first of all， besides， what's more， moreover， in addition， most importantly...

Dear Sam，

Knowing that you are worried about your healthy condition， I am writing this email to make some suggestions.

Firs of all， you _____

_____

_____

_____

_____

_____

I sincerely hope these suggestions may help you live a healthy life. Looking forward to your reply.

Yours,

_____

2. After writing, some students will be invited to share their compositions and the teacher as well as the other students will make some comments.

【Design intention】Through this less-controlled activity, students will be able to integrate what they've learned in previous activities to write an email of advice so that they will have their comprehensive competence developed.

Step 5. Self-assessment.

In this lesson,

1. I have mastered the meaning and usage of modal verbs (ought to, ought not to, have to, don't have to, mustn't and needn't).   Yes./No.

2. I can give suggestions on keeping healthy with modal verbs.   Yes./No.

3. I am able to write the email of advice.   Yes./No.

4. I think I could do better if I...

【Design intention】In this part, students will reflect on what they've learned in this class and know how to make improvements in future learning.

Step 6. Homework.

Individual task: Polish your writing and share it with your classmates.

Group task: Choose one of the situations (in the teachers' office, in the classroom, at home, at a store...) and create a dialogue. Try to use as many modal verbs as possible. You will present your dialogues in the next class.

【Design intention】Homework is used to help students consolidate what they have learned and also apply it to real-life situations.

教学设计二——班级公约

Step 1. Lead-in.

Ask students the following questions to lead the topic:

1. What are the goals of your class?

Possible answers: to build a united, harmonious, and excellent class, etc.

2. To achieve these goals, what should you do to build a better class?

【Design intention】 Two questions are used to inspire students' thoughts of what should do and shouldn't do at school and arouse their subconsciousness of using the modal verbs.

Step 2. Brainstorming.

Ask students to brainstorm what they should do to realize the goals of the class and list students' dos and don'ts on the blackboard.

dos	don'ts
study hard	be lazy
respect the teachers	be disrespectful
get along with classmates	treat classmates in an unkind way
finish the homework on time	attack others without reasons
pay attention to personal hygiene	say mean words to others
take active part in class activities	throw rubbish everywhere
...	...

【Design intention】 A brainstorming is used to expand students' understanding of their responsibility in the class and to lay a solid foundation for the later class convention.

Step 3. Connecting.

Inspire students to connect the use of modal verbs with their ideas with the follow-up questions:

What modal verbs can you use to explain the dos and don'ts clearly to make a class convention?

Among the target modal verbs in this unit, how can they be used in each class rule?

Present the target modal verbs to the class and ask students to tell the differences in their own way.

● ought to/ought not to ——➤ used to say what is/isn't the right thing to do

● have to/don't have to ——➤ used to show that you must do sth/used to give advice or recommend sth

● mustn't/needn't ——➤ used to say that sth is/isn't necessary or very important （sometimes involving a rule or a law）

【Design intention】The follow-up questions are used to inspire students to connect the modal verbs with proper contexts so that they can understand the use of the modal verbs better.

Step 4. Combining.

Ask students to combine the modal verbs with the suggestions to make a class convention.

The teacher can give an example like this：

The Class Convention of Class 1

To build a more harmonious, active, progressive and excellent class, we students of Class 1 have agreed to obey the following rules and regulations.

1. About going to school

We ought to arrive at school before 7：50 a.m.; we ought not to be late than 8：00 a.m.

We have to...

We mustn't...

2. About the classroom performance

We ought to...

We have to...

We needn't...

3. About homework

We ought to...

We have to...

We needn't...

4. About the classroom cleaning

We ought to...

We have to...

We needn't...

【Design intention】In this part, students can further understand the differences among the target modal verbs in different contexts and learn to use them in an appropriate way by combining the target grammar and their real-life needs.

Step 5. Presentation and discussion.

Students present their own version of the class convention and discuss to improve the drafts to make a thorough version.

Give some comments and immediate help when necessary.

【Design intention】In this part, students can practice what they need to master about the modal verbs by presentation and discussion to consolidate their understanding of the target grammar.

Step 6. Homework.

Students are required to add more details to the class convention after they consult with the head teacher.

【Design intention】In this part, students can practice the proper use of modal verbs in their oral expression through in-person communication.

第六章

句法与词法教学设计

第一节　主谓一致

教学设计——生活常识

Step 1. Greetings and lead–in.

1. Do you ever have hiccups（打嗝）? How do you feel when you have hiccups?

2. Why do we have hiccups and what's the cure to stop hiccups?

3. Watch a video *Hiccups* from BBC animation — *Peppa Pig*.

【Design intention】Lead-in from a familiar topic from our daily life will provide the students with an easy atmosphere and the cute animation characters will arouse their learning interest to start this grammar lesson.

Step 2. Observing and analyzing.

Activity 1. Observe the following sample sentences to pay attention to the bold verbs and analyze the relationships between verb formats and their subjects.

1. What is the family doing?

The family is having breakfast.

2. How are Daddy and Mummy Pig having their breakfast?

Daddy and Mummy Pig are having their breakfast slowly.

3. How does Peppa as well as Gorge is having breakfast?

Peppa as well as Gorge is having breakfast very quickly.

4. How does George feel after breakfast?

George has hiccups and there is nothing he can do to stop his hiccups.

Activity 2. Think about the two questions.

1. Compared with Chinese, what should we pay special attention to when we make an English sentence?

The family is having breakfast.

Daddy and Mummy Pig are having their breakfast.

2. Does an English verb keep the same just like Chinese?

【Design intention】Students will have a general acknowledge of rules of subject-verb agreement by observing the sample sentences, and they will build a better understanding of the similarities and differences between English and Chinese through the comparison of the two languages.

Step 3. Practice and consolidation.

Activity 1. Describe the story.

1. George _____ (eat) his breakfast too quickly, so he _____ (have) hiccups.

2. Daddy and Mummy pig _____ (eat) their breakfast slowly so they do not have hiccups.

3. Since it _____ (be) a sunny day, George and Peppa _____ (be) longing to go out to play.

4. The game throw-and-catch the ball _____ (be) very interesting.

5. Neither his parents nor his sister _____ (have) hiccups.

6. A pair of glasses _____ (be) on Daddy pig's nose.

7. All the family except George _____ (be) laughing.

Activity 2. Fill in the blanks with correct verbs in the passage.

Ways to stop hiccups:

1. Nearly 50% hiccups _____ (be) cured by taking a deep breath

repeatedly, which _____ (help) guide the wrong air out of lungs.

2. Someone _____ (think) that drinking a big mouth of cold water and swallowing it slowly _____ (be) a good treatment.

3. Distraction（分散注意力）like watching TV or talking with someone else _____ (be) also a good choice. Thus, that people _____ (use) the way of scaring the hiccuping person _____ (be) reasonable.

4. Not only pushing your middle finger but also pushing your first web（虎口）and pushing the center of eyebrow（眉心）_____ (have) been proved to be good means of curing hiccups.

5. Holding our breath and pulling our tongue as well as breathing into a paper bag _____ (be) good means of stop hiccuping.

Activity 3. Situational dialogue.

Imagine one of your friends begins hiccuping and cannot stop on the way to school, and he/she feels extremely awkward and uncomfortable. Talk with him/her and give a hand to comfort him/her. For example：

A：Hic, hic, hic, ...

B：Oh, poor guy, you are hiccuping all the way. Need any help?

A：Yes, thanks. What shall I do? Hic...

B：...

...

A：Thank you so much！Your cures are quite good！

Activity 4. Free discussion.

Topic：What shall we do if we are in an embarrassing situation?

A：Be ashamed and just avoid facing it and even escape from the situation?

...

B：Accept your bad situation and think positively to find a solution?

【Design intention】In this part, students will have chances to practice the rules of subject-verb agreement in both sentences and passages and in the forms of both oral and written English, when their knowledge will be consolidated gradually and their healthy sense of human body will be strengthened.

Step 4. Conclusion.

1. Hiccuping is such a natural and hard experience that everyone should suffer，thus we should not laugh at someone who is involved in it，but offer a hand to those who are hiccuping.

2. English and Chinese are different in the form of verbs.

Three rules of subject-verb agreement（主谓一致原则）：

Grammatical concord-form of subject（语法一致）

Notional concord-meaning of subject（意义一致）

Principle of proximity-place of subject（就近原则）

3. Live hopefully，and think positively.

【Design intention】In this part，students can view the whole class from a whole angle and build a comprehensive knowledge system of key competence ranging from language ability to thinking quality，from learning ability to culture sense.

Step 5. Homework.

If you were Li Hua，your foreign teacher Professor Smith would give a healthy lecture about hiccups，and he has written to you for collecting some knowledge of this topic. Please write back to offer some helpful information. Requirements are as follows：

1. Your reply should contain both the reasons and the cures of hiccup.

2. You should write at least 100 words but no more than 120 words.

3. Pay attention to the form of verbs in each sentence.

【Design intention】Homework is used to revise and improve students' language ability and helpful to cultivate their divergent thinking as well.

第二节　构词法

教学设计——主题公园

Step 1. A guessing game.

【Design intention】The game is to get students to guess a theme park，which can show students the topic about this grammar learning class. Besides，it aims to stimulate students' enthusiasm in this class.

Step 2. Group work of introducing theme parks.

1. Each group is given one envelop containing pictures and clue words.

2. Discuss in groups of 4 to introduce the theme park using the clue words and pictures.

3. The reporter introduces the theme park to the whole class.

【Design intention】This group work can help students to use the word formation in real language context.

Step 3. Fill in the blanks according to the Chinese.

1. Disneyland.

_____（迪士尼乐园）will bring you into a magical world，whether you are travelling through space，visiting a _____（海盗船）or meeting your favourite _____（童话故事）or cartoon character. As you wander around the fantasy _____（欢乐，娱乐）park，you may see _____（白雪公主）or _____（米老鼠）in a parade or on the street. Of course you can also _____（体验）giant swinging ships and terrifying _____（自由落体）. With all these _____（吸引人的地方），no wonder tourism is increasing _____（无论哪里）there is a Disneyland.

2. Dollywood.

Dollywood shows and celebrates America's _____ （传统的）southeastern culture. People come from all over America to see carpenters and other _____ （工匠/手艺人）make wood, glass and iron objects in the _____ （过时的）way. You can take a ride on the only _____ （蒸汽火车）still working in the southeast of America. Dollywood has one of the best old wooden _____ （过山车）. It is _____ （世界著名的）for having the most length in the smallest space.

【Design intention】In this part, students are expected to fill in the blanks according to the Chinese, which can help students experience the word formation.

Step 4. Make a dialogue.

1. Show students some pictures about the Amusement Park in Ankang.

2. Find some students to describe the Amusement Park in Ankang according to the given pictures.

3. Make a dialogue.

Imagine you are Li Hua. Your pen-pal Tom will come to Ankang to visit the Amusement Park and he wants to know some information about it. Now work in groups to make a dialogue to introduce the Amusement Park in Ankang. You can begin your dialogue like this：

Tom：Hello！I will come to visit the Amusement Park in Ankang. Can you introduce it to me？

Li Hua：Of course. There are many amusements in the park, such as roller coaster, ...

Tom：Wow！That sounds great. And I am wondering what I should do if I am misunderstood by local people.

Li Hua：Don't worry. I will be your guide all the way. And the people here are very friendly.

Tom：That's great. But where can we taste the delicious local food？/ But which transportation I should choose to get there？

Li Hua：...

【Design intention】In this part, students need to describe the Ankang Amusement Park first and then need to make a dialogue by means of pair work.

Step 5. Write a short passage to introduce the Amusement Park in Ankang.

Sample：

The <u>Amusement Park</u> in Ankang lies in Ankang hi-tech zone, in which you can go sightseeing, have fun and enjoy your leisure time. There are many large-scale facilities of <u>recreation</u>, such as the <u>revolving-wood-horses</u>, the <u>roller coaster</u>, <u>the free-fall drops</u>, <u>the pirate ship</u>, <u>5D cinema</u>, etc. You can <u>experience whichever</u> you like. Also you can taste some delicious local snacks there. Besides, it is better to <u>book</u> the ticket <u>online</u> in advance, by which the <u>admission</u> is lower.

【Design intention】In this part students need to write a short passage to describe the Amusement Park in Ankang, which can help students consolidate what they have learned in this class.

第三节　倒装

教学设计一——生活哲理

Step 1. Read the classic sentences and guess the movie.

Long long ago, there was a temple on the hill.

In the temple lived a master.

Master once told the panda A Bao：

Only when you believe you are special, can you make something special.

【Design intention】Some classic sentences are used to introduce the teaching target of this class and arouse students' interest as well.

Step 2. Observe and summarize.

1. Long long ago, there was a temple on the hill.

2. In the temple lived a master.

3. Only when you believe you are special, can you make something special.

Summary: The types and structure of inversion.

Types	Structures
Full inversion	V+S
Partial inversion	Be/do/does/did/can/have/has/had...+V+S

【Design intention】Through observation and discovery, students will have a basic understanding of the types and structures of inversion. Also students can learn one life philosophy — believe you are special.

Step 3. Read the story and find the inverted sentences.

Here comes a story about two scholars. They were on their way to taking the imperial examination. It happened that they saw a funeral procession. No sooner had the first scholar seen the coffin than he felt frustrated. He thought to himself: "In no way will I pass the examination." A coffin stands for bad luck. So pessimistic was he that he failed the exam.

However, the other scholar thought quite differently. He regards the coffin as promotion and wealth. Not only was he extremely delighted but also he did fairly well in the exam. Such an optimistic man was he that he succeeded.

The story tells us that only if we smile to life will life smile at us in return.

According to the above passage, correct the following mistakes first, and then classify the types of inversion and summarize the inversion rules.

1. Here come a story about two scholars.

Here comes a story about two scholars. (full inversion: there/here/prepositional words)

2. No sooner the first scholar seen the coffin than he felt frustrated.

No sooner had the first scholar seen the coffin than he felt frustrated. (partial inversion: no sooner...than...)

197

3. In no way will I passed the examination.

In no way will I pass the examination. （partial inversion：negative words）

4. So pessimistic he that he failed the exam.

So pessimistic was he that he failed the exam. （partial inversion：so...that）

5. Not only he extremely delighted but also he did fairly well in the exam.

Not only was he extremely delighted but also he did fairly well in the exam. （partial inversion：not only...but also...）

6. Such an optimistic man was he that did he succeeded.

Such an optimistic man was he that he succeeded. （partial inversion：such...that）

7. Only if do we smile at life will life smile at us in return.

Only if we smile to life will life smile at us in return. （partial inversion：only+adverbial）

【Design intention】Through reading passage，finding inversions from the passage，correcting mistakes and then summarizing the types and rules of inversion，students will have a comprehensive understanding of inversion. Also students can learn one life philosophy — smile to life and life will smile at you.

Step 4. Practice.

Work in groups of 4 and change the sentences into inverted sentences according to the rules you have summarized.

A story about a rabbit and a tortoise comes now. One day，a tortoise decided to have a race with a rabbit. The rabbit was so proud that he believed he ran fast. He not only teased the tortoise but also told him to quit at first. However, the tortoise never gave up. Then the race began. The rabbit ran so fast that the tortoise couldn't catch up. Then the rabbit slept on the half way. He had hardly slept when the tortoise got ahead of him. The rabbit didn't realize the tortoise had won until he woke up. He felt regretful. If he hadn't slept，he would have won.

It is such a funny story. From this story，we learn that we can do anything successfully only with persistence and modesty.

【Design intention】This activity can not only enable students to practice inversion by changing the sentences, but also train students' oral expression, as well as teaching students one life philosophy — be persistent and modest about everything you do.

Step 5. Writing.

You must have met many difficulties during English study. It is your persistence and modesty that get you where you are now. Please write a short passage to describe your story of learning English and your feelings about it.

Requirement:

1. Please try to use inversion sentences as many as possible.

2. The following structure will be of help to you.

Here comes my story about learning English. _____

_____

_____

_____

So I'm convinced that only with persistence and modesty, can we do anything successfully, let alone learning English.

【Design intention】This step is to give the students another chance to help them consolidate what they have learned in this class and at the same time train students' ability to use English to tell their own study experience.

Step 6. Presentation.

Find some students to share their writing and others try to come up with some suggestions to help solve their difficulties.

Step 7. Homework.

Share your story with your partner to check whether there are some mistakes.

Remember three life philosophies: Believe you are special; smile to life; be persistent and you will succeed one day.

【Design intention】Homework is used to help students consolidate what they have learned and to cultivate students' optimistic life attitude as well.

教学设计二——职业规划

Step 1. Lead-in：Discussion.

We have learned the text— My First Work Assignment "Unforgettable"，says a new journalist. Here comes one question for you：how to be a good journalist?

Below are two short passages about how to be a good journalist. Please read and compare them.

A

One will never be a good journalist unless he has the following qualities.

First and foremost，if he wants to be a qualified journalist，he should be not only well-educated but also experienced so that he can use his professional knowledge and previous experience to deal with various situations he will face. In addition，he must be a curious and active person with good communication skills if he wants to do a good job. That's because there will be various people he needs to deal with and he won't acquire all the information he needs to know if he doesn't ask many different questions. Meanwhile，although he is talkative，he needs to remember to talk less with good manners and listen more with care. Last but not least，he will face so many cases that he can never know when someone will accuse him of getting the wrong end of the stick. So he needs to get the evidence in a legal way to support his story.

B

Never will one be a good journalist unless he has the following qualities.

First and foremost，not only should he be well-educated but also experienced so that he can use his professional knowledge and previous experience to deal with various situations he will face. In addition，only if he is a curious and active person with good communication skills will he do a good job. That's because there will be various people he needs to deal with and only if he asks many different questions will he acquire all the information he needs to know. Meanwhile，talkative as he is, he needs to remember to talk less with good manners and listen more with care. Last but not least, so many cases will he face that never can he know when someone will accuse him of getting the wrong end of the stick. So he needs to get the evidence in a legal way to support his story.

Above are the qualities a good journalist must have. Do you want to be a good journalist?

Can you tell me which is better? And why?

【Design intention】One purpose of this part is to help students review what they have learnt in the reading passage. The other purpose is to introduce the focus of this class with familiar learning materials to lower the difficulty of the grammar point: Partial Inversion.

Step 2. Discuss and imitate.

I have been a teacher for 18 years. So long is it that I often feel there will be still a long way to go. Can you tell me how to be a good teacher in the eyes of the students?

Here comes some sentences. Please analyze them carefully and then imitate to write your own sentences using what you have discussed.

1. Never will one be a good journalist unless he has the following qualities.

_____

2. Not only is he well-educated but he is also experienced so that he can use his professional knowledge and previous experience to deal with the situations he will face.

_____

3. Only if he is a curious and active person with good communication skills will he do a good job.

_____

4. Talkative as he is, he needs to remember to talk less with good manners and listen more with care.

_____

5. So many cases will he face that never can he know when someone will accuse him of getting the wrong end of the stick.

_____

Now please put the sentences together and make a short passage. You can add some details to make it fluent.

【Design intention】The purpose of this part is to develop students' thinking quality and learning ability by discussing the question, analyzing the sentences, and then imitating to write their own sentences. In the end, they are expected to connect all the sentences to make a complete passage to develop their logic thinking ability.

Step 3. Group work: Rewrite.

Thank you for telling me how to be a good teacher. And I will try my best to equip myself with the qualities you have mentioned. Now, as a teacher, I know all of you want to be top students. Here is a passage I wrote to help you grow into a top student. Please read it and then rewrite it using inversion.

Personally, I think one will never be a top student unless he is equipped with the following qualities.

First and foremost, he should be not only hard-working but also persistent, for diligence is the mother of success and it may be so long a period before one can succeed. In addition, although one may be intelligent, if he wants to learn efficiently, he needs to know the right methods of learning, such as preview and revision, self-exploration and cooperation, practice and reflection and so on. Last but not least, one should know there is so much waiting for him to learn. He should never be too proud of his past success. Instead, be modest about his own achievements and always ready to learn from others. Remember, among any three people walking, you will find something to learn for sure.

Such are the qualities a top student should have. Hoping you can be a top student and then be admitted to your dream university.

【Design intention】In this part, students are expected to cooperate with each other to rewrite the passages using partially inverted sentences. In this way, they can learn better with the help of each other. Meanwhile, when they are doing the work, their attitudes towards learning will be positively influenced, which is beneficial to their future study.

Step 4. Individual work：Writing.

We have known how to be a good journalist，a good teacher and a top student. Now please write a passage about how to be a good citizen. When writing，try to use as many inverted sentences as you can.

【Design intention】This part is designed not only to help students have a better and further understanding of partial inversion，but also to develop their sense of social responsibility and to cultivate their patriotism.

Step 5. Presentation.

Several students will be invited to share their writing. The other students and the teacher will make comments on the works.

【Design intention】This part is designed to test whether students have gained the required knowledge，letting students learn from others as well as their own improper expressions and building up their confidence in English learning by showing themselves.

Step 6. Homework.

What kind of job do you want to take？And how to make preparations for it？

教学设计三——社会责任

Step 1. Lead-in.

Read the following news.

At the beginning of March，a BBC reporter named John Sudworth released a series of reports about China，claiming that not only did they find the new evidence of China's moving Uighur minority workers to uproot communities，but also they have collected enough evidence about China's using forced labors in Xinjiang.

1. Is this news true or false from your perspective？

According to some netizens，seldom did BBC news report China in a fair and unbiased way. It was not until the previous report about Xinjiang broadcast four years ago was found by some Chinese people did we realize BBC actually used the old pictures of the previous report combined with the story they made up to make the so-called "news about China".

2. Is this a proper way to make news?

In no way/By no means/At no time/ Under no circumstances should a reporter cover a story without taking justice and fairness into account.

3. What should China do to fight against the western bias towards China?

Actually, China has released a documentary named "Western Media Unlocked—A Xinjiang of Two Tales". However, that's not enough. Only when we Chinese people strive hard to make ourselves equipped with more knowledge and make our country more powerful in every aspect will we have the power to speak for our country and have more opportunities to play an important role in international affairs.

Step 2. Read and summarize.

1.They not only found the new evidence of China's moving Uighur minority workers in order to uproot communities, but also they have collected enough evidence about China's using forced labors in Xinjiang.

Not only did they find the new evidence of China's moving Uighur minority workers in order to uproot communities, but also they have collected enough evidence about China's using forced labors in Xinjiang.

2. We didn't realize BBC actually used the old pictures of the previous report with the story they made up to make the so-called "news about China" until the previous report about Xinjiang broadcast four years ago was found by some Chinese people.

It was not until the previous report about Xinjiang broadcast four years ago was found by some Chinese people did we realize BBC actually used the old pictures of the previous report with the story they made up to make the so-called "news about China".

3. A reporter should never/in no way/by no means/at no time/under no circumstances cover a story without taking justice and fairness into account.

Never/In no way/By no means/At no time/Under no circumstances should a reporter cover a story without taking justice and fairness into account.

4. BBC news seldom report China in a fair and unbiased way.

Seldom did BBC news report China in a fair and unbiased way.

5. We have the power to speak for our country and have more opportunities to play an important role in international affairs only when we Chinese people strive hard to make ourselves equipped with more knowledge and make our country more powerful in every aspect.

Only when we Chinese people strive hard to make ourselves equipped with more knowledge and make our country more powerful in every aspect will we have the power to speak for our country and have more opportunities to play an important role in international affairs.

Summary：

1. Not only + 系动词/助动词/情态动词 + 主语 + …

2. Not until ... + 系动词/助动词/情态动词 + 主语 + …

3. Never/ In no way/By no means/At no time/ Under no circumstances/ Seldom/+ 系动词/助动词/情态动词 + 主语 + …

4. Only after/when + 状语从句，系动词/助动词/情态动词 + 主语 + …

5. So/Such … + 系动词/助动词/情态动词 + 主语 + … + that…

【Design intention】One purpose of this part is to help students review what they have learned in the past. The other purpose is to introduce the focus of this class：Partial Inversion.

Step 3. Practice：Rewrite the following sentences and try to deliver a speech.

Activity 1. Work in groups to rewrite the following sentences by using the partial inversion.

1. You cannot become a good reporter until you are knowledgeable and experienced.

_____

2. A good reporter should not only have the strong curiosity to find out the truth of the story but also have the courage to report a true story.

3. You will acquire all the information that you need to know only when you have the patience and make full preparations.

4. A reporter will never become excellent if he doesn't have a good "nose" for a story.

5. A good reporter will face so many complex situations he has never expected that he has to be cautious and careful enough to avoid falling into danger.

Requirements:

1. The students who rewrite the sentences must use the partial inversion.

2. The students who rewrite the sentences need to explain why they do them in this way.

【Design intention】The purpose of this part is to develop students' thinking quality and learning ability by discussing the question, analyzing the sentences, and writing their own sentences. In the end, they are expected to connect all the sentences to make a complete passage to develop their logic thinking ability.

Activity 2. Discuss with your group members about what qualities make a good reporter.

Nowadays, the news media has a great influence on people's attitude towards many things, including social phenomena, which, to some extent, decide the direction of social development. However, with the rise and popularity of the social media, some reporters distort the fact of the story just to attract more attention or to cater to the public, which has greatly disturbed the normal social order. It seems that how to cultivate qualified reporters and how to regulate the media have become the most urgent problems to be solved. Therefore, how to become a good and qualified reporter?

First and foremost, never will one have the qualification to be a reporter until he equips himself with courage, knowledge and experience.

...

【Design intention】In this part, students are expected to cooperate with each other to rewrite the passages using partially inverted sentences. In this way, they can learn better with the help of each other. Meanwhile, when they are doing the work, their attitudes towards learning will be positively influenced, which is beneficial to their future study.

Step 4. Writing.

Supposing your best friend is going to be a reporter soon, write a letter to him, expressing your congratulations to him, telling him some bad phenomena existing in our society, especially the social media, advising him to be a good reporter and showing your determination to support him.

Attention:

1. Please try to use the partial inversion sentences as many as possible.

2. Every correct sentence is worth 10 points.

【Design intention】This part is designed not only to help students have a better and further understanding of the partial inversion, but also to develop their sense of social responsibility and to cultivate their patriotism.

Step 5. Presentation.

Several students will be invited to share their letters. The other students and the teacher will make comments on the works and also give some advice to help make them better.

【Design intention】This part is designed to test whether students have gained the required knowledge, letting students learn from others as well as their own improper expressions and building up their confidence in English learning by showing themselves.

Step 6. Homework.

Polish your letter and try to learn from your mistakes or improper expressions.

教学设计四——旅游经历

Step 1. Lead-in.

Have an interview with some of the classmates to ask their experiences and feelings if they have visited Beijing before.

Sample questions:

1. Have you ever been to Beijing? What about your deskmate?

2. How much do you know about Beijing?

3. What part of Beijing impresses you most?

4. How can you enjoy yourself in Beijing?

Anticipated answers:

1. I have never been to Beijing. My deskmate hasn't been there, either.

2. I don't know much about Beijing.

3. The old Beijing yogurt is so tasty that it impresses me a lot.

4. We can know more about Beijing only by travelling there and experiencing the food and culture on our own.

Magic time:

Change the sentences above into sentences containing the inversion.

1. Never have I been to Beijing, nor has my deskmate.

2. Little do I know about Beijing.

3. So tasty is the old Beijing yogurt that it impresses me a lot.

4. Only by travelling there and experiencing the food and culture on our own can we know more about Beijing.

【Design intention】An interview is used to arouse students' familiar knowledge and also refresh their minds using the new grammar, and make students feel the power of the inversion at the same time.

Step 2. Observe and analyze.

Ask students to observe the sentences above and ask students to analyze the similarities and characteristics of them.

Then introduce the new grammar knowledge — Partial Inversion.

Ask students to summarize the rules of the inversion from the sentences and make some complements when necessary.

Suggested answers:

1. Negative adverbs like nor, neither, never, hardly, seldom, rarely, scarcely, nowhere, few, etc. are put at the beginning of the sentence.

2. Negative phrases such as by no means, under no circumstances, in no case, at no time, etc. are put at the beginning of the sentence.

3. The structures of only followed by prepositional phrase, adverbs of time or adverbial clauses are put at the beginning of the sentence.

4. Inversion can be used in some special structures like so/such … that…, not only... but also, not...until..., as/though, etc.

【Design intention】Observation, analysis and summary are required for students to have a general and systematic knowledge of the partial inversion.

Step 3. Pair interview.

Ask students to interview their classmates about the following cities: Beijing, Shanghai, New York, London, while the use of inversion in their expressions is mandatory. Then ask the interviewer to retell the interviewee's experiences and feelings.

【Design intention】This part aims to involve students in practicing the inversion by connecting with their own life to strengthen their understanding of the grammar.

Step 4. Report.

Students report their classmates' travel experiences and feelings using the inversion to emphasize their thoughts.

Expected answers:

Never has my deskmate been to Beijing before. However, by no means does it mean that he knows little about Beijing. On the contrary, he has told me so much about Beijing. Beijing is the capital of China. Not only does it have modern buildings, but it also has many places of interest, like the Great Wall. It is said that only if we reach the Great Wall can we be called a true man. Besides, we can't miss the Beijing roast duck, which is very delicious. Once we have a taste of it, never will we forget its flavor. Such a charming city is Beijing that it draws a large number of visitors from home and abroad every year. Though he reads this on the magazine, it still has left a deep impression on him.

【Design intention】By reporting their classmates' travel experiences, students can have a better idea of how the inversion works in oral English.

Step 5. Comments and reminders.

Give students comments on their reports and remind students the key points on how to use inversion correctly.

Then summarize the class using the following sentences:

Only by travelling and reading can we enrich our mind; only when you realize how travel changes your inner sides will you fully feel the charm of it; only then will you realize that this world has too much to offer to us.

Step 6. Homework: Writing a travel experience.

Ask students to write a short passage about one of their travel destinations using inversion properly.

【Design intention】A travel experience passage writing is designed to consolidate students' mastery of inversion and also evaluate their proficiency and accuracy in using inversion.

第四节　省略

教学设计一——校园生活

Step 1. Read the speech loudly and try to leave out the unnecessary parts in underlined sentences in groups.

Good morning, dear classmates. As Mr. Liu <u>said that</u> we need to decorate our classroom last week, we need to discuss the decoration plan and we need to choose an appropriate plan. Actually, we all don't like the way that the classroom is decorated without any consideration. If the classroom is well-decorated, the classroom will offer us a better place to study. My job is to collect your plans, to discuss with you and to prepare related materials. If it is possible, let's cooperate with each other to put forward an acceptable and an available plan. I hope that each group can take an active part in it.

【Design intention】 The purpose of reading the speech and leaving out the unnecessary parts is to arouse students interest. Meanwhile, students are expected to find out the unnecessary parts to introduce the teaching target— ellipsis in this class.

Step 2. Work in pairs to rewrite the underlined sentences using ellipsis, and compose a more concise speech and finally read it out.

Eg: As Mr. Liu said that we need to decorate our classroom last week, ...

—→ As Mr. Liu said we need to decorate our classroom last week, ...

【Design intention】 By rewriting the speech, students will have a basic understanding of ellipsis. During this period, students are encouraged to be familiar with the structure as well. By reading more concise speech, students will understand how to put it into practical use.

Step 3. Read and act.

Activity 1. Group work.

Read the dialogue, rewrite it using ellipsis and do a role-play after rewriting it.

Monitor: Come on, every group leader. Your plans are warmly welcomed.

Group One: If it is so, our group members think that we can attach more inspiring pictures on the wall.

Group Two: If it is possible, we assume that we can change the way that we place the desks.

Group Three: If it is necessary, we consider that we can buy some green plants.

Monitor: If we together decorate the classroom more beautiful, we will feel more comfortable.

Please rewrite the dialogue using ellipsis as below.

Monitor: Come on, every group leader. Your plans are warmly welcomed.

Group One: If so, our group members think that we can attach more inspiring pictures on the wall.

Activity 2. Free talk.

If you were invited to share your ideas, would you please come up with more suggestions to decorate our classroom?

Attention:

Please try your best to use ellipsis.

Eg 1: If possible/necessary/so/not, we can...

Eg 2: If decorated with more flowers, the classroom will...

Eg 3: Given me a chance to decorate our classroom, I will...

Eg 4: Imagining us sitting in a nice-looking classroom, we are bound to do sth.

Eg 5: Our classroom can be decorated in western or eastern style, for example...

【Design intention】For the activity 1, by rewriting the dialogue cooperatively, students will be provided the related context to learn the structure of ellipsis effectively. For the activity 2, students are offered a chance to consolidate what they've internalized and digested. Hence, students will be provided opportunities to learn how to use ellipsis effectively in an open atmosphere by independent thinking. At the same time they are encouraged to take an active part in the activities.

Step 4. Practice.

Activity. Work in groups to offer suggestions again and do an interview.

(Students take turns to act as Monitor.)

An interview:

Monitor: Thank you for your participation. Can you share your idea with us?

Student A: Sure. If _____, I think _____.

Monitor: What about you?

Student B: _____ (fill) with books, the classroom _____.

Monitor: Your suggestion?

Student C: Certainly. _____ (think) of the basketball stars, I can do nothing buy wait.

Monitor：How about your ideas?

Student D：Seeing cartoons _____（hang）in our classroom，I have no choice but to study more enthusiastically.

Monitor：Thanks for your sharing.

Attention：

The students who put forward suggestions are expected to use ellipsis.

【Design intention】By filling in the blanks in pairs，students will be provided the related context to check if they really know the structures of ellipsis and then internalize the grammar themselves. By performing the interview，students are offered a chance to consolidate what they've internalized. At the same time they are inspired to think about their own inner thoughts，thus arousing their desire to share their ideas.

Step 5. Writing.

If you were the monitor，after listening to the stated suggestions，you would deliver a conclusion speech about the classroom-decoration idea and the plan. Please compose a conclusion speech.

Attention：

1. Please try to use ellipsis as much as possible.

2. Every correct ellipsis is worth 10 points.

【Design intention】This part is designed to help students to put what they have learned into practical use. Meanwhile，students are expected to express themselves in English correctly by using the grammar，which is indispensable for them to form an English thinking mode and understand the difference between Chinese and English better.

Step 6. Presentation.

Two students are invited to share their speech and others try to make a correction and give scores they deserve.

Step 7. Homework.

Polish your speech and share it with your desk mate and ask him/her to give you some advice.

教学设计二——急救

Step 1. Lead-in：A first aid quiz.

First aid is a contemporary form of help given to someone who suddenly falls ill or gets injured before a doctor can be found. Nowadays there are a lot of unexpected accidents. Let's see if the following ways are proper ways to deal with the emergency? If not, explain the reasons and find out better ways.

1. If having a hurt ankle, you can put an ice pack on your ankle and not put a heating pad around it.（Right.）

2. When getting a nosebleed, gently let your head back to stop the bleeding.（Wrong. It may lead the blood into the throat and easily cause choking.）

3. To treat a burn, you hold the burnt part under cold running water and then rub（擦）some butter on it.（Wrong. The first step is right but the second step is not.）

4. Your friend has an asthma（哮喘）attack, but doesn't have her medicine. You'd better get her a cup of coffee.（Right, because caffeine can help to dilate the windpipe.）

5. To treat a choke, you should make him/her spit by patting him/her on the back.（Right.）

【Design intention】One purpose of this part is to help students review what they have learned in this unit. The other purpose is to introduce the focus of this class with familiar learning materials to lower the difficulty of the grammar point—ellipsis.

Step 2. Read and summarize.

1. First aid is a contemporary form of help given to someone who suddenly falls ill or gets injured before a doctor can be found.

2. If not, explain the reasons and find out better ways.

3. If having a hurt ankle, you can put an ice pack on your ankle and not put a heating pad around it.

4. When getting a nosebleed，gently let your head back to stop the bleeding.

5. It may lead the blood into the throat and easily cause choking.

6. To treat a burn，you hold the burnt part under cold running water and then rub some butter on it.

7. The first step is right but the second step is not.

8. Your friend has an asthma（哮喘）attack，but doesn't have her medicine. You'd better get her a cup of coffee.

Summary：

1. First aid is a contemporary form of help（which/that is）given to someone who suddenly falls ill or gets injured before a doctor can be found.

First aid is a contemporary form of help given to someone who suddenly falls ill or gets injured before a doctor can be found.

2. If（they are）not（proper ways），explain the reasons and find out better ways.

If not，explain the reasons and find out better ways.

3. If（you are）having a hurt ankle，you can put an ice pack on your ankle and （you can）not put a heating pad around it.

If having a hurt ankle，you can put an ice pack on your ankle and not put a heating pad around it.

4. When（you are）getting a nosebleed，gently let your head back to stop the bleeding.

When getting a nosebleed，gently let your head back to stop the bleeding.

5. It may lead the blood into the throat and（it may）easily cause choking.

It may lead the blood into the throat and easily cause choking.

6. To treat a burn，you hold the burnt part under cold running water and then （you）rub some butter on it.

To treat a burn，you hold the burnt part under cold running water and then rub some butter on it.

7. The first step is right but the second step is not（right）.

The first step is right but the second step is not.

8. Your friend has an asthma（哮喘）attack，but（your friend）doesn't have

her medicine. You'd better get her a cup of coffee.

Your friend has an asthma（哮喘）attack，but doesn't have her medicine. You'd better get her a cup of coffee.

【Design intention】The purpose of this part is to develop students' thinking quality and learning ability by discussing the question and analyzing the sentences.

Step 3. Group work：Rewrite.

Activity 1. Work in groups to rewrite the following sentences using ellipsis according to the given information in the envelop.

1. Stay away from the boiling water or you can get burnt by hot liquids and you can get burned by steam. The burn that one gets will be red and will be painful.

_____

2. If you do get burnt accidentally，tie a bandage firmly over the burnt area，when a bandage is necessary.

_____

3. Luckily，if the burns are not serious，they should feel better with a day or two.

_____

4. These burns affect the top layer of the skin and they also affect the second layer of the skin.

_____

5. If your nose is bleeding，you should bend forward so that the blood runs out of your nose and the blood doesn't run down your throat.

_____

6. If someone is suffering a snake bite，he/she should be kept still and unmoved. Do not wash the venom off the skin or try to suck out the venom.

_____

7. If you find someone's ankle sprained，have the victim sit down and elevate the foot. Put an ice pack on the ankle to reduce the swelling and put a firm bandage around the foot and ankle.

_____

8. First aid, if it is quickly and correctly given, can save a person's life.

Activity 2. Discuss with your group members about what you would advise if given a chance to deliver a speech about first aid to the students learning at school.

Example:

Nowadays there are a lot of unexpected accidents. Having a knowledge of first aid can save our lives in an emergency. Therefore, what should we do to prevent ourselves from being hurt or even being killed if something dangerous happens?

First and foremost, stay away from the boiling water or you can get burnt by hot liquids or steam. The burn that one gets will be red and painful.

...

【Design intention】 In this part, students are expected to rewrite the sentences using ellipsis. In this way, they can learn better with the help of each other. Meanwhile, when doing the work, their attitudes towards learning will be positively influenced, which is beneficial to their future study.

Step 4. Individual work: Writing.

We all know that electricity, fire, water, gas, etc. play an important and essential role in our daily life. However, they can be dangerous at some points, so raising people's awareness of protecting themselves and equipping people with a knowledge of first aid seem urgent at the moment.

Supposing you are an experienced doctor, give some advice on first aid to students at school and to their parents in order to help them know more about first aid.

【Design intention】 This part is designed not only to help students have a better and further understanding of ellipsis, but also to develop their sense of social responsibility.

Step 5. Presentation.

Several students will be invited to share their advice. The other students and the teacher listen carefully.

Step **6**. Homework.

Share more advice on first aid among your classmates after class and also you can surf on the Internet to find more useful knowledge about it.

参考文献：

［1］中华人民共和国教育部.普通高中英语课程标准（2017年版2020年修订）［S］.北京：人民教育出版社，2020.

［2］梅德明，王蔷.普通高中英语课程标准（2017年版2020年修订）解读［M］北京：高等教育出版社，2020.

［3］中华人民共和国教育部.普通高中英语课程方案（2017年版2020年修订）［S］.北京：人民教育出版社，2020.

［4］中华人民共和国教育部考试中心.中国高考评价体系［M］北京：人民教育出版社，2019.

［5］中华人民共和国教育部考试中心.中国高考评价体系说明［M］北京：人民教育出版社，2019.

［6］陈静静.学习共同体——走向深度学习［M］.上海：华东师范大学出版社，2020.

［7］何亚男，应晓球.高中英语语法教学活动设计［M］上海：上海教育出版社，2011.

［8］王兰英.对六要素整合的高中英语学习活动观的认识和实践［J］.中小学外语教学（中学篇），2018（12）：7-12.

［9］朱尧平.活动观与质量观兼行：英语课程深度教学的实现［J］.教学与管理，2019（6）：107-109.

［10］刘科.英语活动观视角下教师课堂角色构建研究：表现与启示［J］.中小学教师培训，2019（11）：68-72.

［11］韩旭.基于学习活动观的高中英语教学现状及对策研究［D］.延吉：延边大学，2020.

［12］刘正芳、尹恒.主题意义引领下的高中英语语法教学——以定语从句教学为例［J］.中小学英语教学与研究，2020（07）：67-69.

［13］许秋娟.在主题意义探究过程中实施英语语法教学的实践［J］.中小

学英语教学与研究，2020（09）：55-60.

［14］赵习美、杨晓钰. 英语学习活动观视角下的高中语法教学新途径
［J］. 英语学习，2020（11）：49-54.

［15］王蔷，钱小芳，吴昊. 指向英语学科核心素养的英语学习活动观—内
涵、架构、优势、学理基础及实践初效［J］. 中小学外语教学，2021
（7）：1-6.

［16］吴迪. 活动理论视域下的英语课堂创新素养教育［J］. 中小学外语教
学，2021（8）：18-23.

［17］蓝海莲. 落实学习活动观，融双语文化能力培养于高中英语语法课堂
［J］. 英语教师，2021（9）：21-24.

［18］程瑞. 学习活动观指导下的高中英语语法教学研究［J］. 英语教师，
2021（10）：161-163.

［19］赵岳瑜. 基于学习活动观的PPP语法教学模式探究［J］. 中学生英
语，2021（12）：74-75.

结语

你我同行，春暖花开

当我突然从眼前的世界惊醒时，才发现窗外已经是霓虹闪烁，车水马龙。电脑页面上鼠标指针仍然在闪烁，一个个英语单词组成密密麻麻的矩阵，传递出厚实而又繁复的气息。我突然意识到，这种视觉上的动静很是相宜，出入其中，很容易忘我。

反复滚动着鼠标，一遍遍检视书中收录的所有教学设计，从理念到流程，从板块到章节，从设计到用意，甚至每一个标点符号，这种感觉就像在抚摸自己的孩子。每一个教学设计的形成都经过了精雕细琢，多少次夜不能寐，多少次辗转反侧，只是想让"她"更好一点，再好一点，与自己的初衷再接近一点。有时仅是为了某一个例句，会在半夜披衣而起，打开电脑忙活好半天。有时候灵感突至，便会断然放下手头上的要紧事，翻出笔记本奋笔疾书。是的，很长一段时间里，工作之余，"她"几乎是我的全部。

事非经过不知难。众里寻"她"千百度，踏破铁鞋，背后的辛酸当然是冷暖自知。这漫漫长路上，我也曾"理智"地享受着生活的波澜不惊，在自己编织的舒适圈里恬然自安。那时的我，更没有发现自己有什么宏伟的抱负，下意识里，我反倒是不断告诉自己：努力，那是别人的事，我就安安心心做一个小女人吧！然而，当我带领着身边的小伙伴们一路走来，看着她们一点点收获，一步步成长，一项项奖励接踵而来，一本本火红的荣誉证书映照着她们兴奋的脸庞。她们眼中的那种纯粹的感激之情，那种抑制不住的喜悦，是如此的真实而又美好。我的脑海中也开始出现一个声音，萦绕不去。那声音搅扰着我，刺激着我，让我不得安宁，也似乎在一点点催动着我再往前走一步，再走一步……。著名演员王千源有句话说的很好："不疯魔，不成活。我很享受这种若隐若现中的左右徘徊，这是我的选择，也是我想要的语境。"确实如此，我们都在不断打造自己的语境，左右徘徊固然可忧，但经历挣扎与彷徨，当踏平坎坷、历经艰辛，蜕变却绝对是一种享受。回首来路，致敬曾经的自己，深信未来更有无限风景。

抓铁须有痕，踏石必留印。我们的教育工作来不得半点虚假，同样，钻研学问也容不得一丝一毫的敷衍。这些年来，虽然积累了不少一手资料，却始终升不起出书的念头，或者就算偶尔冒出这一想法，也会很快不知所终。不得不说，繁忙的工作确实会淹没很多想法。

再次回顾这些年来一次次的课堂实践，一次次的课后反思，核心素养、英语学习活动观、深度学习……当这些概念一一从眼前闪过，这些年的每一次钻研、实践有如影视中的闪回接连出现。

初见之时，我们很多人确实有过短暂的热情，也想在自己的课堂中进行实践，甚至欲图彻底改变自己的课堂样态。然而，热情过后，一切又会归于平静，因为改变毕竟是一件痛苦的事情，若没有足够的回报，谁愿意做那些无谓的努力呢？于是，就像很多年前的一首老歌唱的那样："山也还是那道山，河也还是那道河。"课堂还是那个课堂，书本还是那些书本，该怎么样还是怎么样。实话实说，我很沮丧于这样的教师生活状态，因为它使人丧失斗志，久而久之犹如行尸走肉，成为一个没有灵魂的空壳子。教师若没有自己的思想与追求，又怎么能够教出有思想、有追求的学生呢？

我常常在想这是不是一个无解的魔咒，为什么教师们参加了那么多培训，听了那么多示范课，可就是不见改变呢？

直到有一个周末，那是一个没课的周日，初秋的清晨，天气出奇的好，我戴着耳机，享受着公园清新的空气，呼吸着树叶里散发的负离子，心情十分舒畅。这时耳机里传来两段话，令我甚为感慨，于是就记录下来：

My success just evolved from working hard at the business at hand each day.

——Johnny Carson

这是美国著名主持人强尼·卡森的获奖感言，讲的是我们每一个人要想成功，必须立足于自己的本职工作，只有日复一日做好本职工作，才会在平凡中孕育伟大。这使我想到我们的英语教研工作一定要为我们的日常英语教学服务，要以提高我们的高中英语教学效果为出发点，而日常的教学实践又会反哺我们的英语教研。那一刻，我突然想到，所谓的本职工作，心心念念的教学突破在长久的时间消磨中正有走向机械重复的趋势，当懵懂代替热情，当"完成教学任务"取代育人追求，长此以往，职业生涯必然只是疲于奔命，价值选择也必将黯然无光。那一刻，我无比期待改变。而另一句萧伯纳的话更是发人深省。

A reasonable man adapts himself to the world, while an unreasonable man persists that the world adapts to himself. However, the progress of human beings is driven by unreasonable people.

——Bernard Shaw

理智的人使自己适应这个世界，不理智的人却硬要世界适应自己。而人类的进步却是由不理智的人推动的。

——萧伯纳

萧伯纳这句看似俏皮的名言却在告诉我们，一个人既要理智地生活、工作，又要超越理智，做一些本不敢做抑或不愿意做的事情。唯有如此，才会有所成就，甚至推动人类的进步。

我觉得教师工作亦是如此，日复一日，年复一年，兢兢业业，一丝不苟。我希望自己或者所有的教师都能成为一盏灯，照亮别人也照亮自己。当情怀与理智交融，当工作与使命共振，平凡的教师也可以有激越的人生，一束微光也可以散发出恒久的力量。

这两段话成了我激励小伙伴们的口头禅。当然，它们也是用来激励自己的。经师教知识，人师教做人，名师著书立说，大师为天地立心，为生民立命。我不敢奢求自己成为名师大师，但我至少应该努力成为人师，我要用自己的言行举止为自己的学生树立一个榜样。我们不是经常激励学生要勤学不辍、奋斗不休吗？作为教师，我又岂能坐井观天、故步自封！

另一个让我下定决心出一本书的诱因是在最近两年，我有幸两次参加了陕西省学科带头人培训，见到了很多英语专业领域的大师，每天与优秀的人在一起，进行着思想上的碰撞和理念上的更新。白天参加培训，晚上打开笔记本回忆学习内容，一边回顾，一边敲敲打打，渐渐地有了汇集一本小书的想法，我不敢称之为专著，就是一本小书而已。

英语新课改有一句我特别喜欢的口号：Tell me，I'll forget；show me，I'll remember；involve me，I'll learn.

其实这句话不仅在课堂上有用，对于英语教师个人的素养提升同样适用。只有让教师们亲自参与到新课程改革、新理念实践、新方法的创建与尝试中，他们才能真正接受新理念、新方法。为了解决目前高中英语语法教学耗时低效的现状，助力广大一线教师在日常教学中更好地践行和落实英语学科核心素养，使学习活动观和深度学习理念在课堂教学中真正得以贯彻和实践，从而促使学生的学习在课堂教学中真实发生，笔者以建构主义理论、合作学习、最近发展区、英语学习活动观和深度学习为理论基础，以高中英语必修课本中的23个语法项目为研究对象，精心设计了五十多个教学课例，努力践行《普通高中英语课程标准（2017年版2020年修订）》中的"英语学习活动观"思想。之所以要出版这本《核心素养视域下的高中英语语法教学研究》，是因为我想让更多的英语教师看到其实这样的教学设计自己也能构思，这样的课堂活动自己也可以设计，这样的课堂氛围自己也可以营造。一旦某些想法与自己的想法产生交集，并让人觉得其实并没有多么难时，接下来的事也就顺理成章、水到渠成了。

不过，很多个夜晚，我辗转难眠，心里似乎有两个小人在打架——一个小人告诉我冲一把，把这本书做出来；另一个小人说还是算了吧，太劳心了。实话实说，做抉择是一件痛苦的事情。然而，心里多少有些不甘。回想这些年自己走过的路，从一个学经济的非师范生到教师，刚站上讲台，可谓诚惶诚恐；从胆战心惊、逐渐成熟、心中有底到小有名气，最后终于能够独当一面。

幸运的是，在我的身边，有一群非常可爱的同伴！她们说不上一呼百应，但无疑是志同道合。我选择的这条道路注定漫长，若是独行，只怕步履维艰。于是，她们迎着光而来，也一起散发出绵延的光。在这里，我想向她们致以最真挚的感谢，如勤于思考的向菊昌、聪明好问的龚雅婷、耐心细致的李如、努力上进的刘欢、任劳任怨的潘燕、温和谦让的张冬梅、干练利索的王楷、稳重务实的闵静、温柔可人的党叶叶、性格开朗的谭力、踏实认真的张玉平、兢兢业业的李媚和专业扎实的陈新莉等。

英语学习活动观主张我们的英语课堂活动设计要遵循一种主题语境，而在我看来，我们英语教师每一天的教学行为都是一种教育表达，这其实同样需要一种语境。与骏马同行，我们的语境是驰骋草原；与春风同行，我们的语境是抚慰大地；与卓越的人同行，我们的语境是拒绝平庸；与善良的人同行，我们的语境是如沐春风。

我，是一个内心温暖的人，读这本书，你我同行，我希望，我们的语境是春暖花开。